THE
NORTON SCORES

An Anthology for Listening

Third Edition • Expanded

Volume II

D0043963

THE

NORTON SCORES

An Anthology for Listening

THIRD EDITION · EXPANDED
IN TWO VOLUMES

VOLUME II:
SCHUBERT TO DAVIDOVSKY

EDITED BY

ROGER KAMIEN

ASSOCIATE PROFESSOR OF MUSIC, QUEENS COLLEGE
OF THE CITY UNIVERSITY OF NEW YORK

W · W · NORTON & COMPANY · INC ·
New York

Acknowledgments

The text for item 1 is from *The Ring of Words* by Philip L. Miller. Reprinted by permission of Doubleday & Company, Inc., and Philip L. Miller.

The scores for items 12 (vocal selection), 13, 14, and 19 are reprinted by permission of G. Schirmer, Inc.

The scores for items 22 and 35 are reprinted by permission of C. F. Peters Corporation.

The score for item 23 is reprinted by permission of Boelke-Bomart, Inc.

The scores for items 24 and 32 are reprinted by permission of Theodore Presser Company.

The scores for items 25, 26, 27, and 31 are reprinted by permission of Boosey and Hawkes, Inc.

The scores for items 28, 30, and 34 are reprinted by permission of Universal Edition A.G.

The score for item 29 is reprinted by permission of Colfranc Music Publishing Corp.

The score for item 33 is reprinted by permission of Associated Music Publishers.

The text for item 35 is from Federico Garcia Lorca, *Selected Poems*. Copyright 1955 by New Directions Publishing Corporation. Reprinted by permission of New Directions Publishing Corporation.

The score for item 36 is reprinted by permission of McGinnis & Marx Music Publishers.

Copyright © 1977, 1970, 1968 by W. W. Norton & Company, Inc.

PRINTED IN THE UNITED STATES OF AMERICA

All Rights Reserved

Library of Congress Catalog Card No

Library of Congress Cataloging in Publication Data
Kamien, Roger, comp.
   The Norton scores.
   Includes indexes.
   CONTENTS: v. 1. Gregorian chant to Beethoven.—
v. 2. Schubert to Davidovsky.
   1. Music—Analysis, appreciation. I. Title.
MT6.K22N7 1977b   780'.15   76-52467
ISBN 0-393-02199-8 (v. 2)
ISBN 0-393-09123-6 (v. 2) pbk.

1 2 3 4 5 6 7 8 9 0

Contents

Preface

This anthology is designed for use in introductory music courses, where the ability to read music is not a prerequisite. The unique system of highlighting employed in this book enables students to follow full orchestral scores after about one hour of instruction. This system also has the advantage of permitting students who *can* read music to perceive every aspect of the score. It is felt that our system of highlighting will be of greater pedagogical value than artificially condensed scores, which restrict the student's vision to pre-selected elements of the music. The use of scores in introductory courses makes the student's listening experience more intense and meaningful, and permits the instructor to discuss music in greater depth.

The works included in this anthology have been chosen from among those most frequently studied in introductory courses. The selections range from Gregorian chant to the present day, and represent a wide variety of forms, genres, and performing media. In this Third Edition, increased emphasis has been placed on music of earlier periods and on music of the present century. A majority of the pieces are given in their entirety, while the others are represented by complete movements or sections particularly suitable for classroom study. Scenes from operas and some choral works are presented in vocal score, while all others are reprinted in their full original form. This anthology may be used independently, or along with any introductory text. The publishers have prepared a set of recordings to accompany *The Norton Scores*.

A few words about the highlighting system employed in the full scores: Each system of score is covered with a light gray screen, and the most prominent line in the music at any given point is spotlighted by a white band (see No. 1 in sample on page x). In cases where two or more simultaneous lines are equally prominent, they are each highlighted. When a musical line continues from one system or page to the next, the white highlighting band ends with a wedge shape at the right-hand margin, and its continuation begins with a reverse wedge shape (see No. 2 in sample). By following these white bands in sequence through the score, the listener will perceive the notes corresponding to the most audible lines. Naturally, the highlighting will not *always* correspond with the most prominent instruments in a specific recording, for performances differ in their emphasis of particular lines. In such cases, we have highlighted those parts that, in our opinion, *should* emerge most clearly. (There are occasional passages in complex twentieth-century works where no single line represents the musical continuity. In such passages we have drawn the listener's attention to the most audible musical events while endeavoring to keep the highlighting as simple as possible.) To facilitate the following of highlighted scores, a narrow white band running the full width of the page has been placed between systems when there is more than one on a page.

It must be emphasized that we do not seek here to *analyze* melodic structure, contrapuntal texture, or any other aspect of the music. The highlighting may break off before the end of a phrase when the entrance of another part is more audible, and during long-held notes the attention will usually be drawn to more rhythmically active parts. The highlighting technique has been used primarily for instrumental music; in vocal works, the text printed under the music provides a firm guideline for the novice score-reader.

A few suggestions for the use of this anthology may be found useful:

1. The rudiments of musical notation should be introduced with a view to preparing the student to associate audible melodic contours with their written equivalents. It is more important for the beginning student to recognize rising and falling lines, and long and short notes, than to identify specific pitches or rhythms. It is helpful to explain the function of a tie, and the layout of a full score.

2. Before listening to a work, it is best for the student to familiarize himself with the names and abbreviations for instruments used in that particular score (a glossary of instrumental names and abbreviations will be found at the conclusion of the book). We have retained the Italian, German, French, and English names used in the scores reproduced in this anthology. This exposure to a wide range of terminology will prepare the student for later encounters with scores.

3. The student should be careful to notice whether there is more than one system on a page of score. He should be alerted for tempo changes, repeat signs, and *da capo* indications. Since performances often differ, it is helpful for the instructor to forewarn the class about the specific repeats made or not made in the recordings used for listening.

4. When a piece is very fast or difficult, it is helpful to listen once without a score.

5. It is best to begin with music that is relatively simple to follow: e.g. (in approximate order of difficulty) Schubert, *An Sylvia;* the second movement of Vivaldi's *Concerto Grosso in D minor*, Opus 3, No. 11; the

first and third movements of Mozart's *Eine kleine Nachtmusik;* the Air from Bach's *Suite No. 3 in D major;* and the second movement of Haydn's *Symphony No. 94 in G major (Surprise).*

6. Important thematic material and passages that are difficult to follow should be pointed out in advance and played either on the recording or at the piano. (We have found that rapid sections featuring two simultaneously highlighted instruments sometimes present difficulties for the students—e.g. Beethoven, *Symphony No. 5,* first movement, m. 65 ff., and Mozart, *Symphony No. 40,* first movement, m. 72 ff.)

We have attempted to keep the highlighted bands simple in shape while showing as much of the essential slurs and dynamic indication as possible. Occasionally, because of the layout of the original score, stray stems and slurs will intrude upon the white area and instrumental directions will be excluded from the highlighting. (Naturally, the beginning of a highlighted area will not always carry a dynamic or similar indication, as the indication may have occurred measures earlier when the instrument in question was not the most prominent.) As the student becomes more experienced in following the scores, he can be encouraged to direct his attention outside the highlighted areas, and with practice should eventually develop the skill to read conventional scores.

I should like to record here my great debt to the late Nathan Broder, who originated the system of highlighting employed here and whose advice and counsel were invaluable. My thanks go also to Mr. David Hamilton, and to Claire Brook and Hinda Keller Farber of W. W. Norton, for many helpful suggestions. I am most grateful to my wife, Anita, who worked with me on every aspect of the book. She is truly the co-editor of this anthology.

R.K.

How to Follow the Highlighted Scores

1. The most prominent line in the music at any given time is highlighted by a white band.

2. When a musical line continues from one system (group of staffs) or page to the next, the white highlighted band ends with a wedge shape, and its continuation begins with a reverse wedge shape.

3. By following the highlighted bands in sequence through the score, the listener will perceive the notes corresponding to the most audible lines.

4. A narrow white band running the full width of the page separates one system from another when there is more than one on a page. It is very important to be alert for these separating bands.

5. When two or more lines are equally prominent, they are each highlighted. When encountering such passages for the first time, it is sometimes best to focus on only one of the lines.

THE

NORTON SCORES

An Anthology for Listening

Third Edition • Expanded

Volume II

1. FRANZ SCHUBERT (1797-1828),
Erlkönig (1815)

Wer reitet so spät durch Nacht
   und Wind?
Es ist der Vater mit seinem Kind;
er hat den Knaben wohl in dem Arm,
er fasst ihn sicher, er hält ihn warm.

"Mein Sohn, was birgst du so bang dein
   Gesicht?"
"Siehst, Vater, du den Erlkönig nicht?
den Erlenkönig mit Kron' und Schweif?"
"Mein Sohn, es ist ein Nebelstreif."

"Du liebes Kind, komm, geh' mit mir!
gar schöne Spiele spiel' ich mit dir;
manch' bunte Blumen sind an dem Strand;
meine Mutter hat manch' gülden Gewand."

"Mein Vater, mein Vater, und hörest du
   nicht,
was Erlenkönig mir leise verspricht?"
"Sei ruhig, bleibe ruhig, mein Kind;
in dürren Blättern säuselt der Wind."

"Willst, feiner Knabe, du mit mir geh'n?
meine Töchter sollen dich warten schön;
meine Töchter führen den nächtlichen
   Reih'n
und wiegen und tanzen und singen dich ein."

"Mein Vater, mein Vater, und siehst du nicht
   dort
Erlkönigs Töchter am düstern Ort?"
"Mein Sohn, mein Sohn, ich seh' es genau,
es scheinen die alten Weiden so grau."

"Ich liebe dich, mich reizt deine schöne
   Gestalt,
und bist du nicht willig, so brauch' ich
   Gewalt."
"Mein Vater, mein Vater, jetzt fasst er
   mich an!
Erlkönig hat mir ein Leid's gethan!"

Dem Vater grauset's, er reitet geschwind,
er hält in Armen das ächzende Kind,
erreicht den Hof mit Müh' und Noth:
in seinem Armen das Kind war todt!

JOHANN WOLFGANG VON GOETHE

Who rides so late through the night
   and the wind?
It is the father with his child;
he folds the boy close in his arms,
he clasps him securely, he holds him warmly.

'My son, who do you hide your face so
   anxiously?"
"Father, don't you see the Erlking?
The Erlking with his crown and his train?"
"My son, it is a streak of mist."

"Dear child, come, go with me!
I'll play the prettiest games with you.
Many colored flowers grow along the shore;
my mother has many golden garments."

"My father, my father, and don't you
   hear
the Erlking whispering promises to me?"
"Be quiet, stay quiet, my child;
the wind is rustling in the dead leaves."

"My handsome boy, will you come with me?
My daughters shall wait upon you;
my daughters lead off in the dance every
   night,
and cradle and dance and sing you to sleep."

"My father, my father, and don't you
   see there
the Erlking's daughters in the shadows?"
"My son, my son, I see it clearly;
the old willows look so gray."

"I love you, your beautiful figure
   delights me!
And if you are not willing, then I
   shall use force!"
"My father, my father, now he is taking
   hold of me!
The Erlking has hurt me!"

The father shudders, he rides swiftly on;
he holds in his arms the groaning child,
he reaches the courtyard weary and anxious:
in his arms the child was dead.

PHILIP L. MILLER

2. SCHUBERT, *An Sylvia* (1826)

Translation

Was ist Sylvia, saget an,
    dass sie die weite Flur preist?
Schön und zart seh' ich sie nah'n,
    auf Himmels Gunst und Spur weis't,
dass ihr Alles unterthan,
dass ihr Alles unterthan.

Ist sie schön und gut dazu?
    Reiz labt wie milde Kindheit;
Ihrem Aug' eilt Amor zu,
    dort heilt er seine Blindheit,
und verweilt in süsser Ruh',
und verweilt in süsser Ruh'.

Darum Sylvia tön', o Sang,
    der holden Sylvia Ehren!
Jeden Reiz besiegt sie lang,
    den Erde kann gewähren:
Kränze ihr und Saitenklang,
Kränze ihr und Saitenklang.

Who is Sylvia? What is she,
    That all our swains commend her?
Holy, fair and wise is she;
    The heaven such grace did lend her,
That she might admired be,
That she might admired be.

Is she kind as she is fair?
    For beauty lives with kindness:
Love doth to her eyes repair,
    To help him of his blindness;
And, being helped, inhabits there,
And, being helped, inhabits there.

Then to Sylvia let us sing,
    That Sylvia is excelling;
She excels each mortal thing
    Upon the dull earth dwelling;
To her let us garlands bring,
To her let us garlands bring.

3. SCHUBERT, Fourth movement (Theme and Variations) from *Quintet in A major (Trout)* for Violin, Viola, Cello, Double Bass, and Piano (1819?)

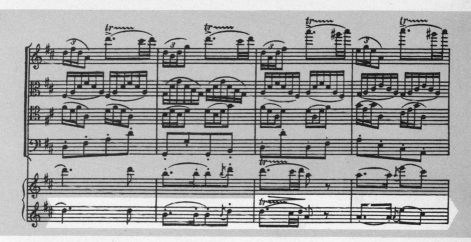

4. HECTOR BERLIOZ (1803-1869),
Fourth movement from *Symphonie fantastique* (1830)

March to the Gallows

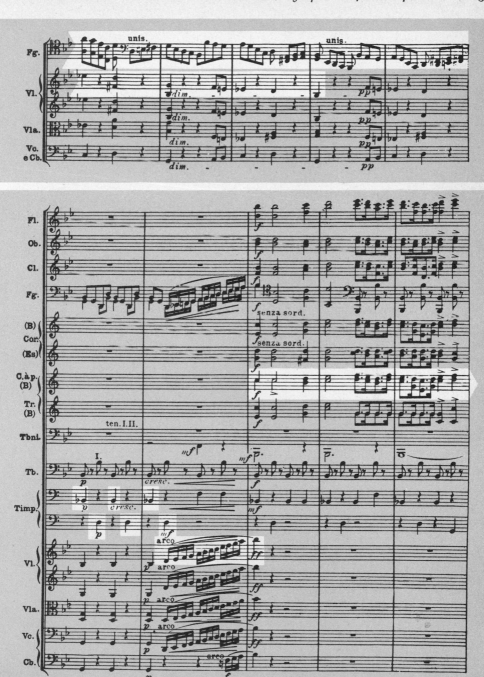

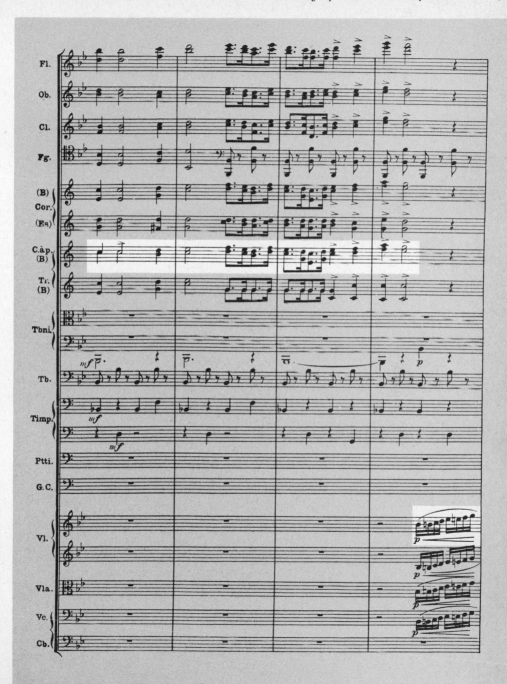

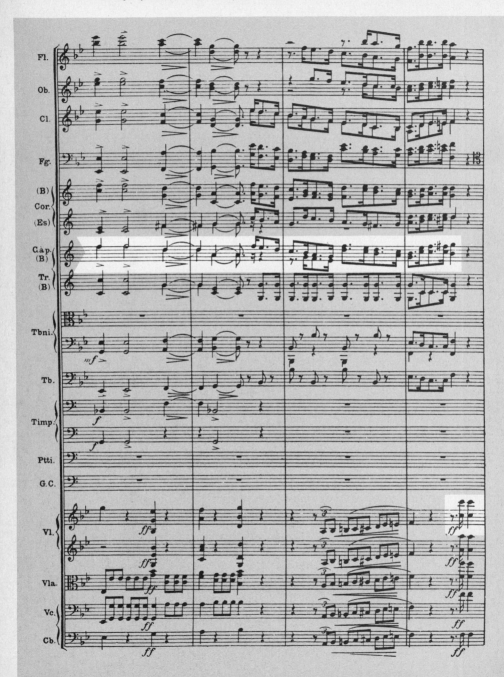

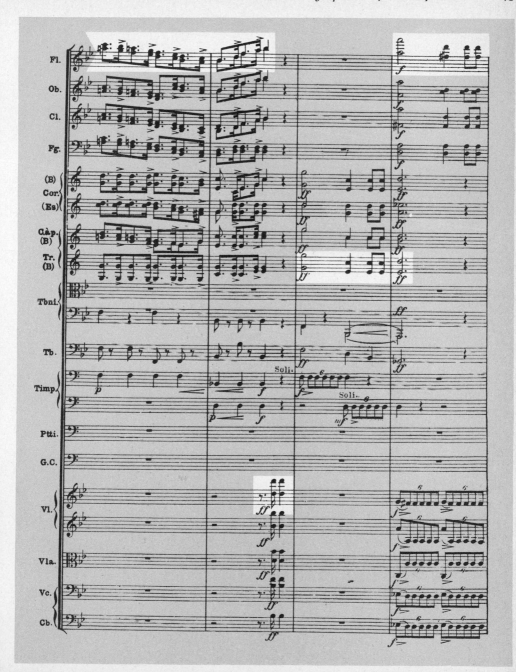

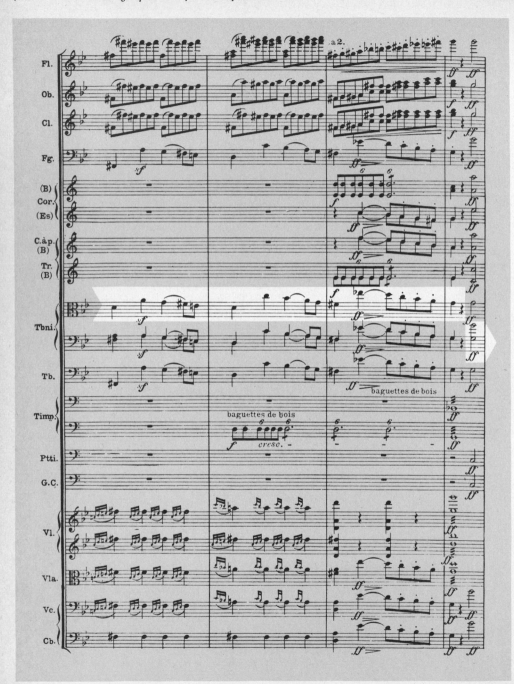

Fl.
Ob.
Cl.
Fg.
(B) Cor. (Es)
C.à p. (B)
Tr. (B)
Tbni.
Tb.
Timp.
Ptti.
G.C.
Vl.
Vla.
Vc.
Cb.
a 2.
dim.
dimin.
f
mf
muta B in H.

Fl.
Ob.
Cl.
Fg.
(B)
Cor.
(Es)
Càp.
(B)
Tr.
(B)
Tbni.
Tb.
Timp.
Ptti.
G. C.
Vl.
Vla.
Vc.
Cb.
a 2.
p
pp
ff

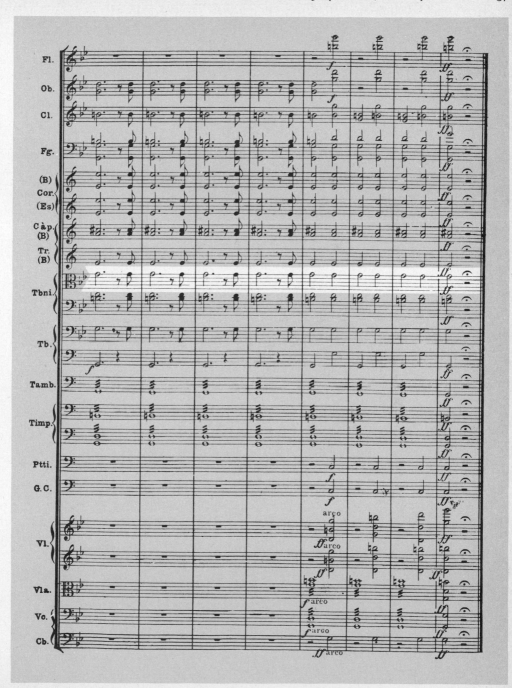

5. FELIX MENDELSSOHN (1809-1847),
Overture to *A Midsummer Night's Dream* (1826)

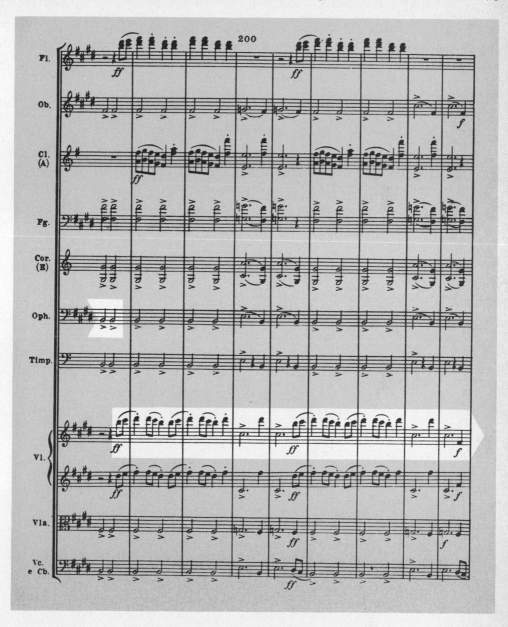

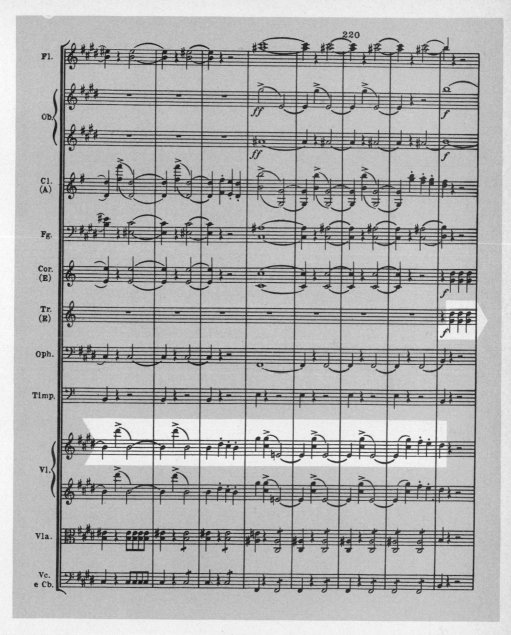

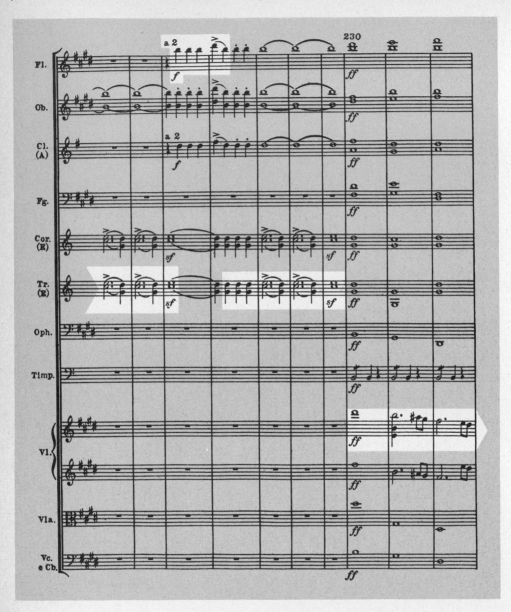

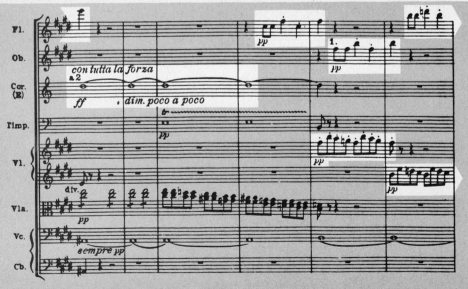

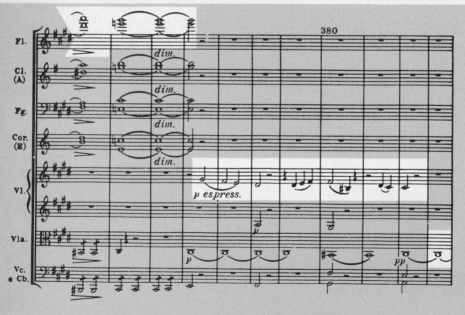

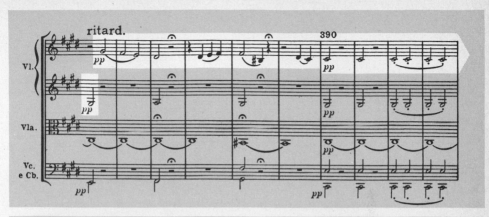

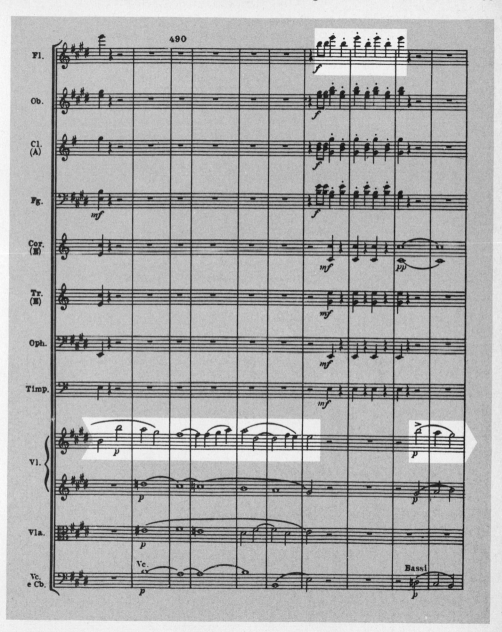

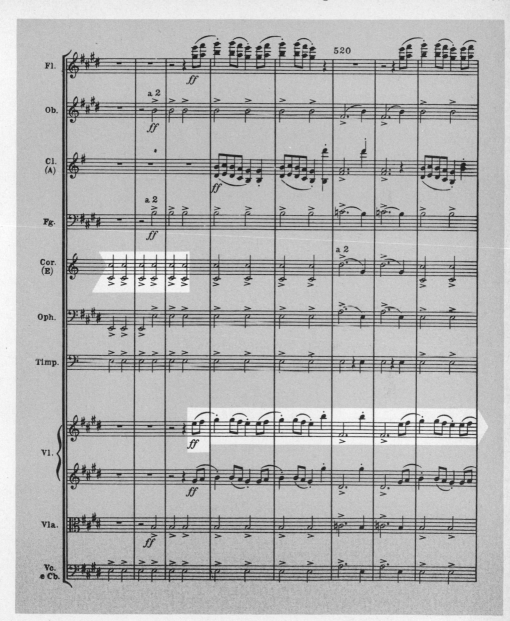

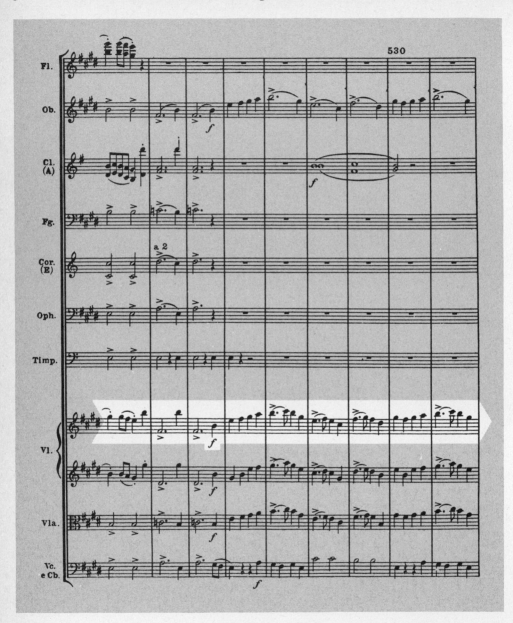

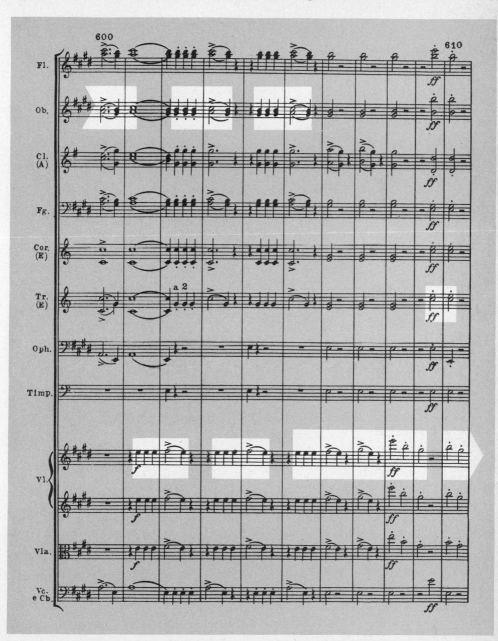

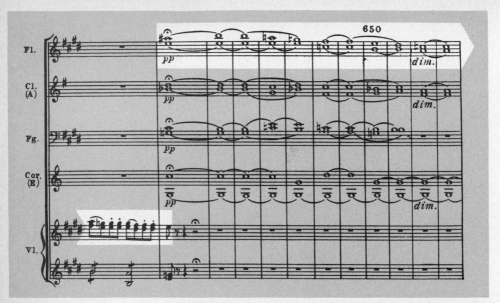

6. MENDELSSOHN,
First movement from *Violin Concerto in E minor* (1844)

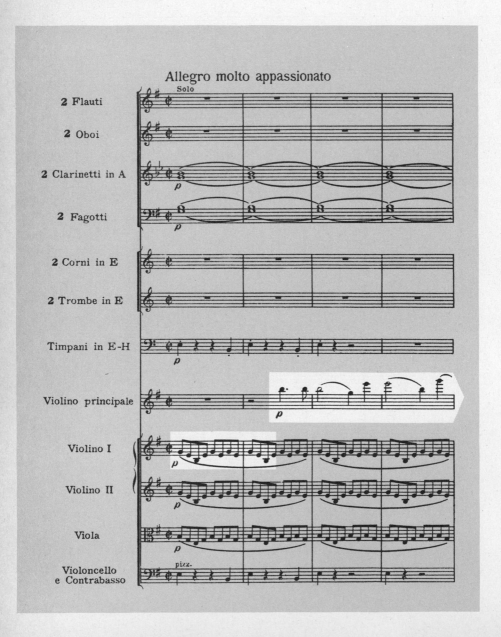

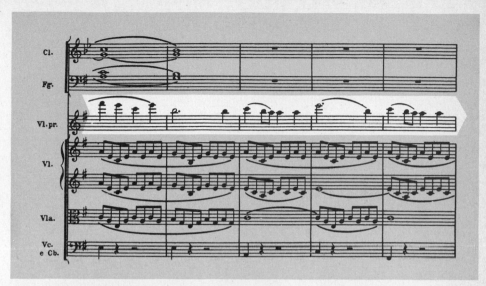

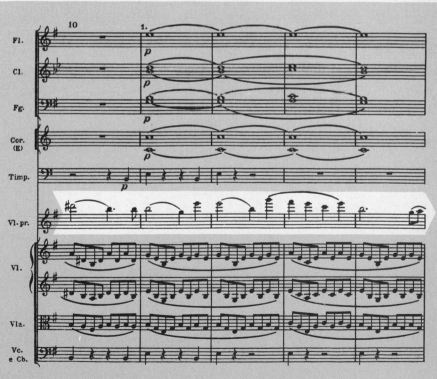

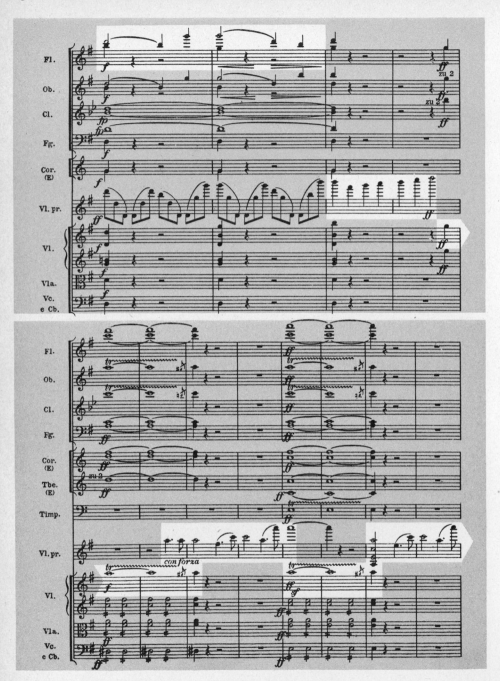

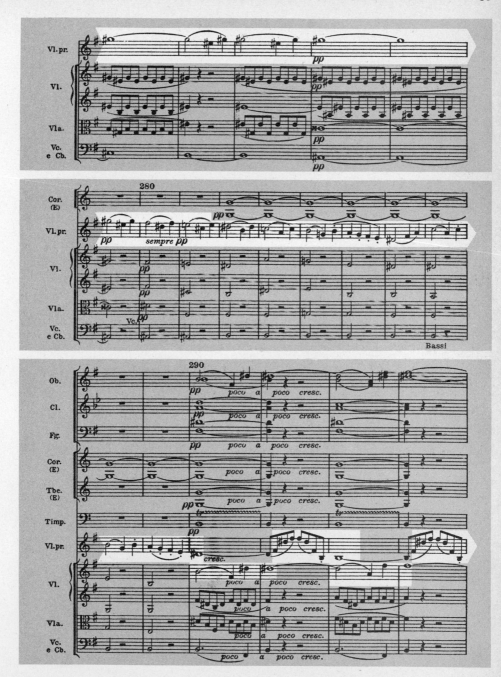

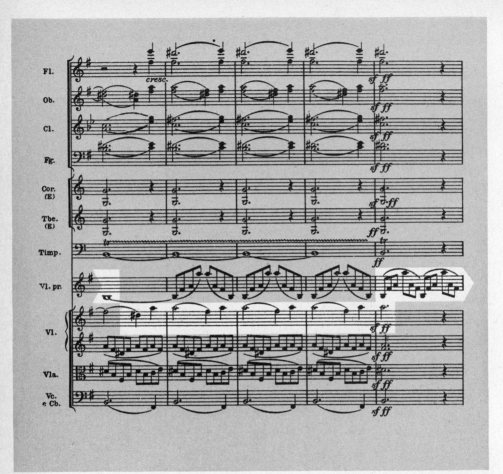

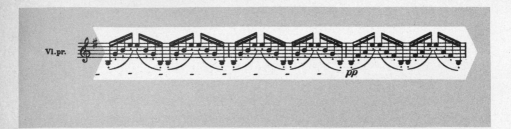

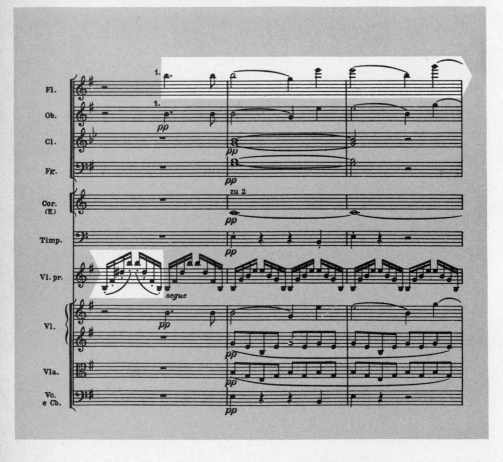

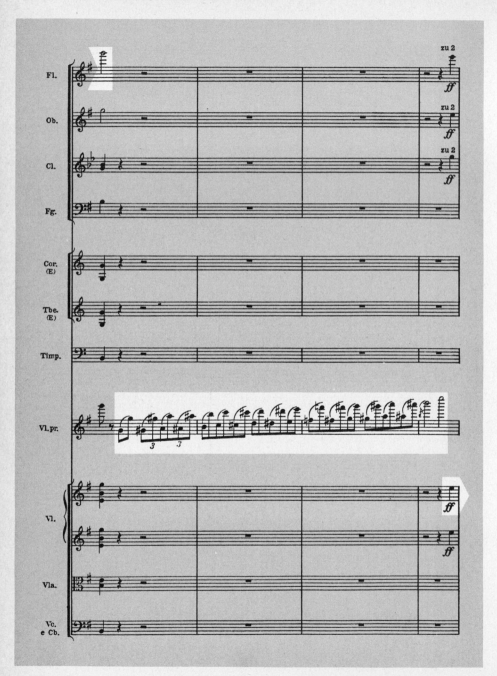

7. FRÉDÉRIC FRANÇOIS CHOPIN (1810-1849),
Mazurka in C-sharp minor, Opus 6, No. 2 (PUBL. 1832)

8. CHOPIN, *Etude in A minor,* Opus 25, No. 11 (PUBL. 1837)

9. CHOPIN, *Prelude in E minor,* Opus 28, No. 4 (PUBL. 1839)

10. ROBERT SCHUMANN (1810-1856),
Mondnacht from *Liederkreis,* Opus 39 (1840)

Translation

Es war, als hätt' der Himmel
  die Erde still geküsst,
dass sie im Blüthenschimmer
  von ihm nur träumen müsst'.
	It seemed as if heaven
	  Quietly kissed the earth,
	So that mid the shimmering blossoms
	  She must dream only of him.

Die Luft ging durch die Felder,
  die Aehren wogten sacht,
es rauschten leis' die Wälder,
  so sternklar war die Nacht.
	A breeze floated through the fields,
	  The stalks of corn waved lightly;
	The forest leaves murmured gently,
	  And starlit was the night.

Und miene Seele spannte
  weit ihre Flügel aus,
flog durch die stillen Lande,
  als flöge sie nach Haus.
	And my soul boldly
	  Outspread her wings,
	Floated over the quiet earth,
	  As if homeward bound.

11. FRANZ LISZT, (1811-1886),
Sonetto 104 del Petrarca (PUBL. 1858)

12. RICHARD WAGNER (1813-1883),
Excerpts from *Tristan und Isolde* (1859)

Prelude

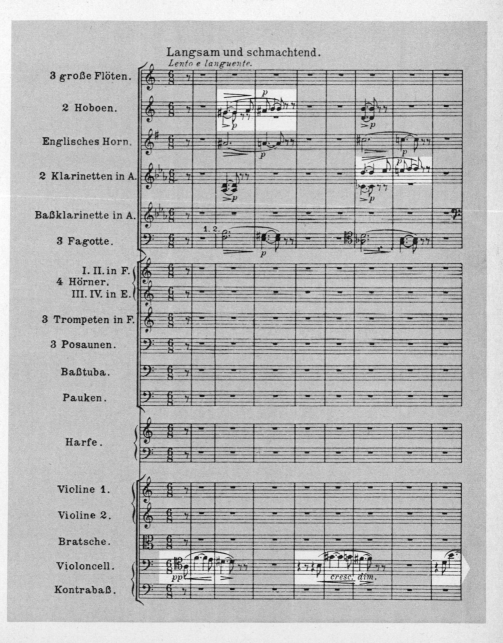

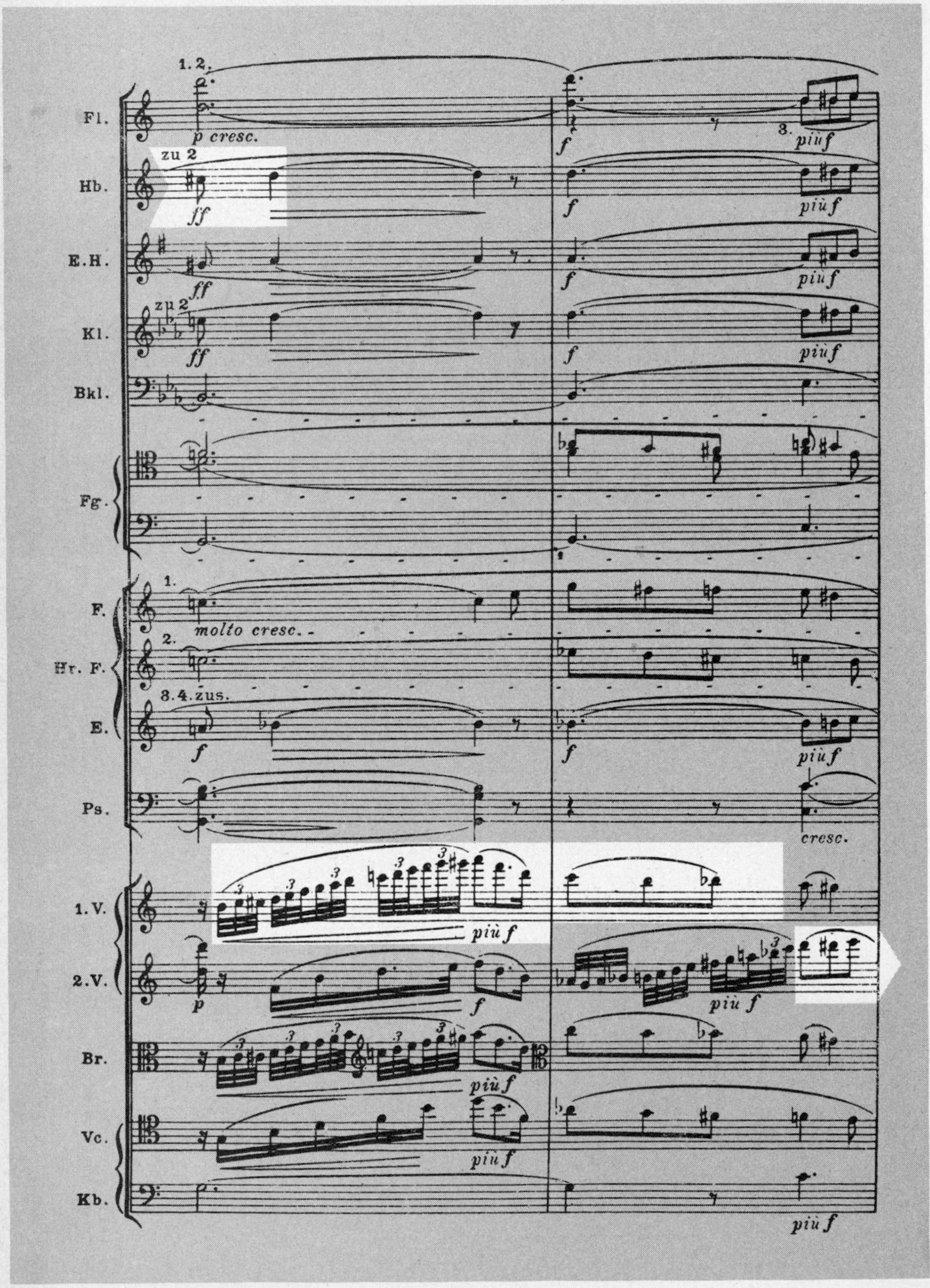
Fl.
1.2.
p cresc.
3.
più f
Hb.
zu 2
ff
E.H.
Kl.
Bkl.
Fg.
F.
Hr. F.
E.
1.
molto cresc.
2.
3.4. zus.
Ps.
cresc.
1. V.
2. V.
Br.
Vc.
Kb.
f
più f

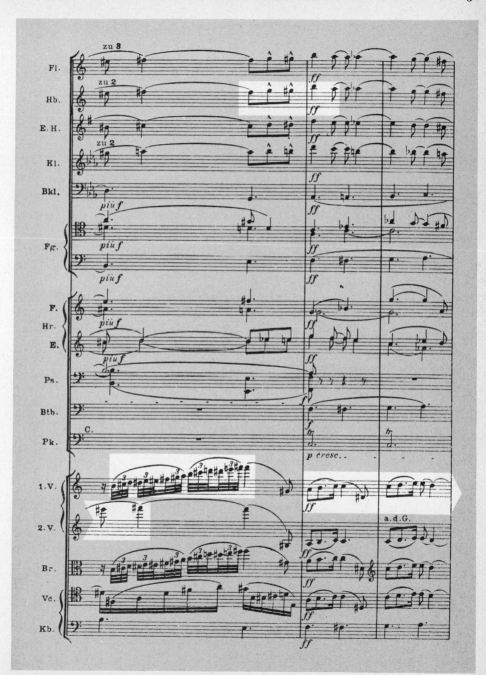

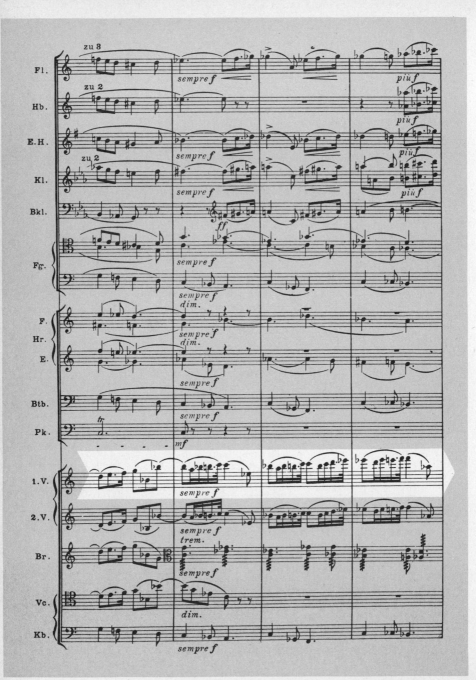

Act II, *Liebesnacht*

Copyright, 1906, by G. Schirmer, Inc. Copyright renewal assigned, 1934, to G. Schirmer, Inc.

Used by permission.

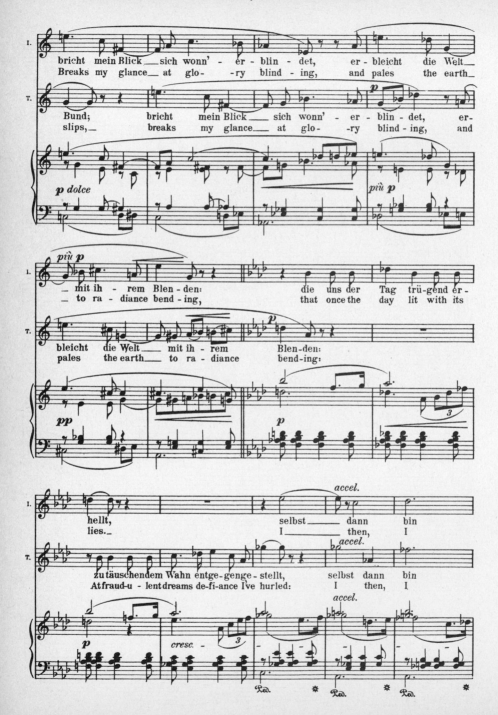

(Completely carried away. Tristan and Isolda sink down and remain lying on the flowery bank, their heads side by side)

Brangæna (from the turret, invisible)

13. GIUSEPPE VERDI (1813-1901),
Violetta's scene from *La traviata*, Act I (1853)

© MCMXLVI, MCMLXI, by G. Schirmer, Inc. Used by permission.

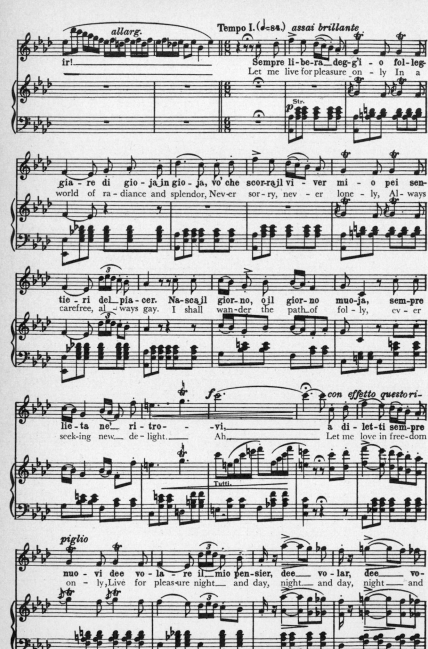

14. VERDI, Opening of the Dies irae from
Messa da Requiem (1874)

Copyright, 1895. by G. Schirmer, Inc.   Used by permission.

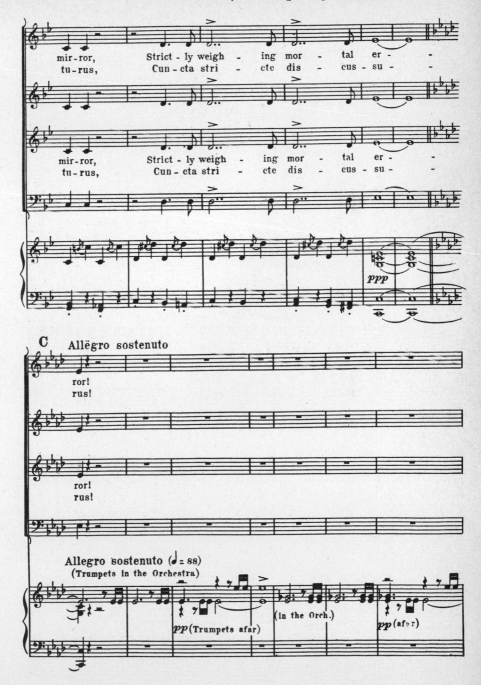

15. JOHANNES BRAHMS (1833-1897),
Third movement from *Symphony No. 3 in F major* (1883)

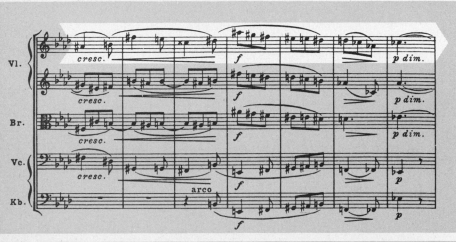

16. MODEST MUSORGSKY (1839-1881),
Boris's monologue from *Boris Godunov*, Act II (1st perf. 1874)

tyázh - kii moi grekh - vis - py - tán - ye, Vin - ói vsekh - zoi men -
pun - ish my crime, still un - par - don'd, my peo - ple lay them

ya na - re ká - yut, klya - nút na posh-chad yákh___ Im - ya Bo - rí - sa!
all at my door. In the mar - ket and the street,___ Bo - ris is ac - curs-ed!

I dá - zhe son be - zhít... iv súm - ra - ke
Now sleep has flown from me... In night's dark-est

nó - chi Dit - ya ok - ro - vái len - no - ye vsta - yót.
hours___ the child De - me - trius comes in blood - stain'd shroud.

17. PETER ILYICH TCHAIKOVSKY (1840-1893), *Romeo and Juliet*, Overture-Fantasy (1869)

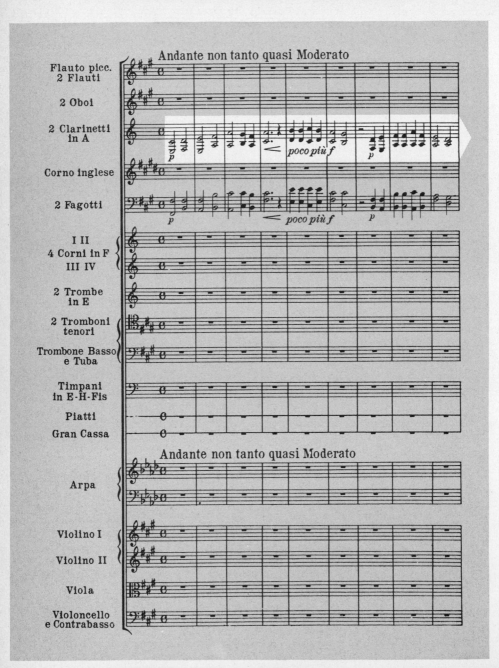

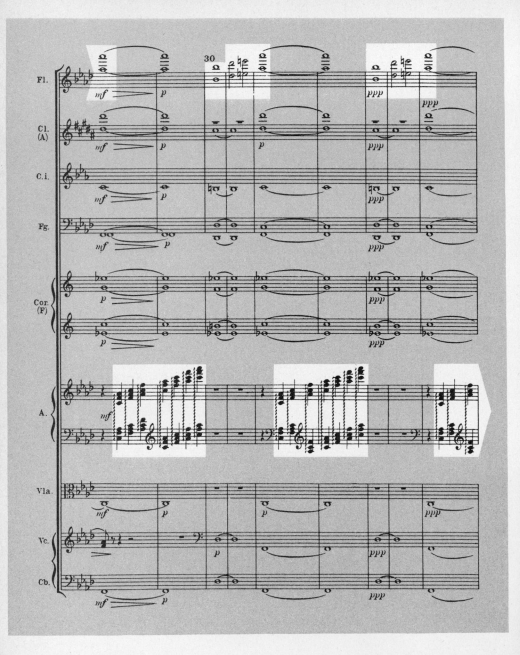

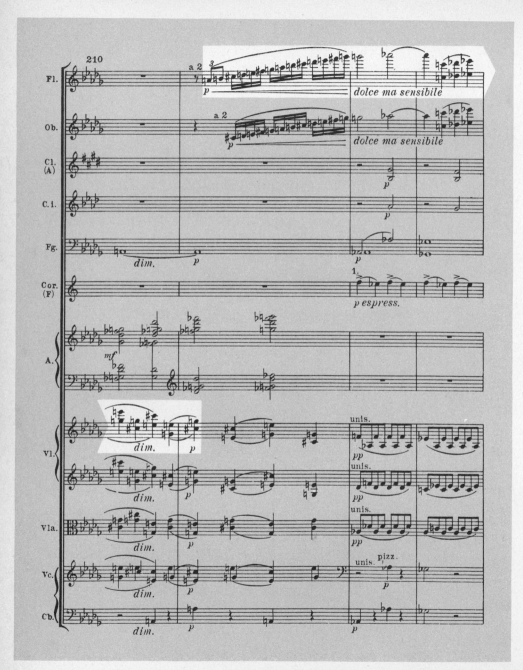

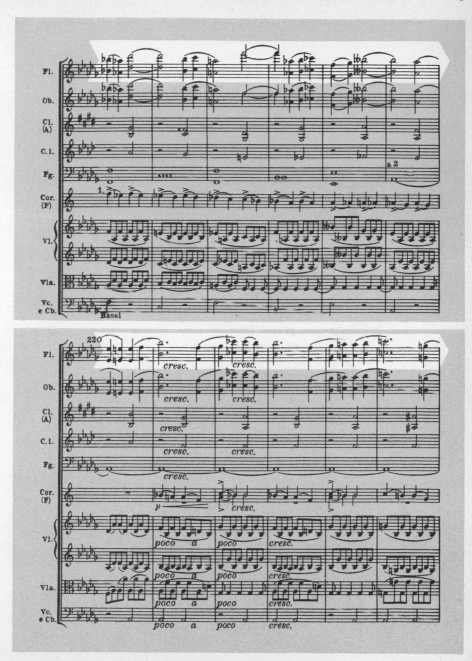

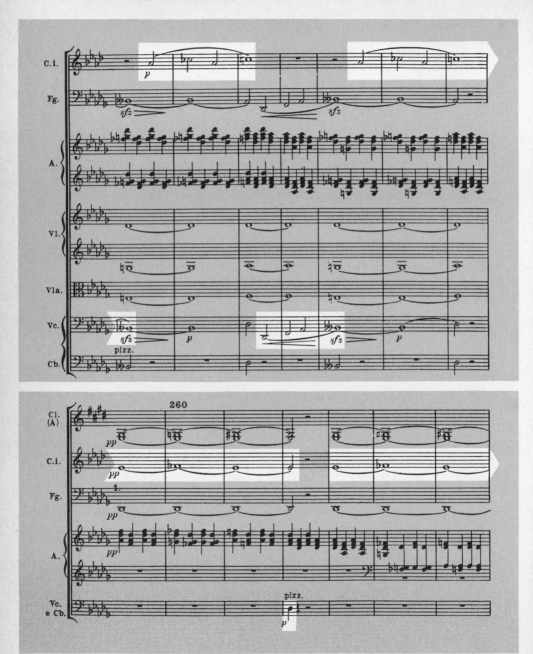

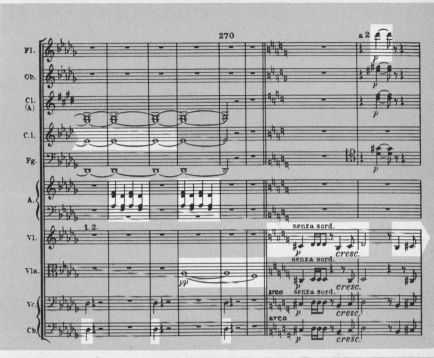

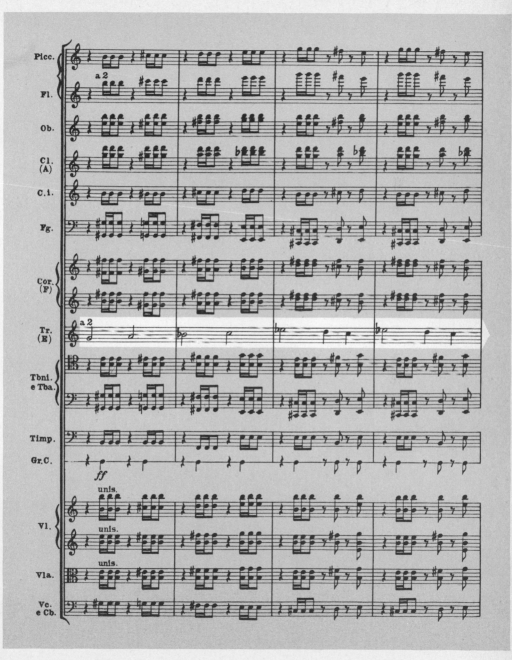

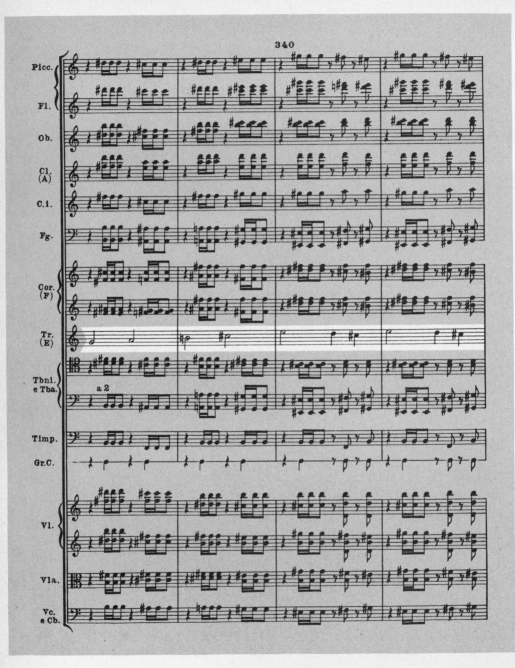

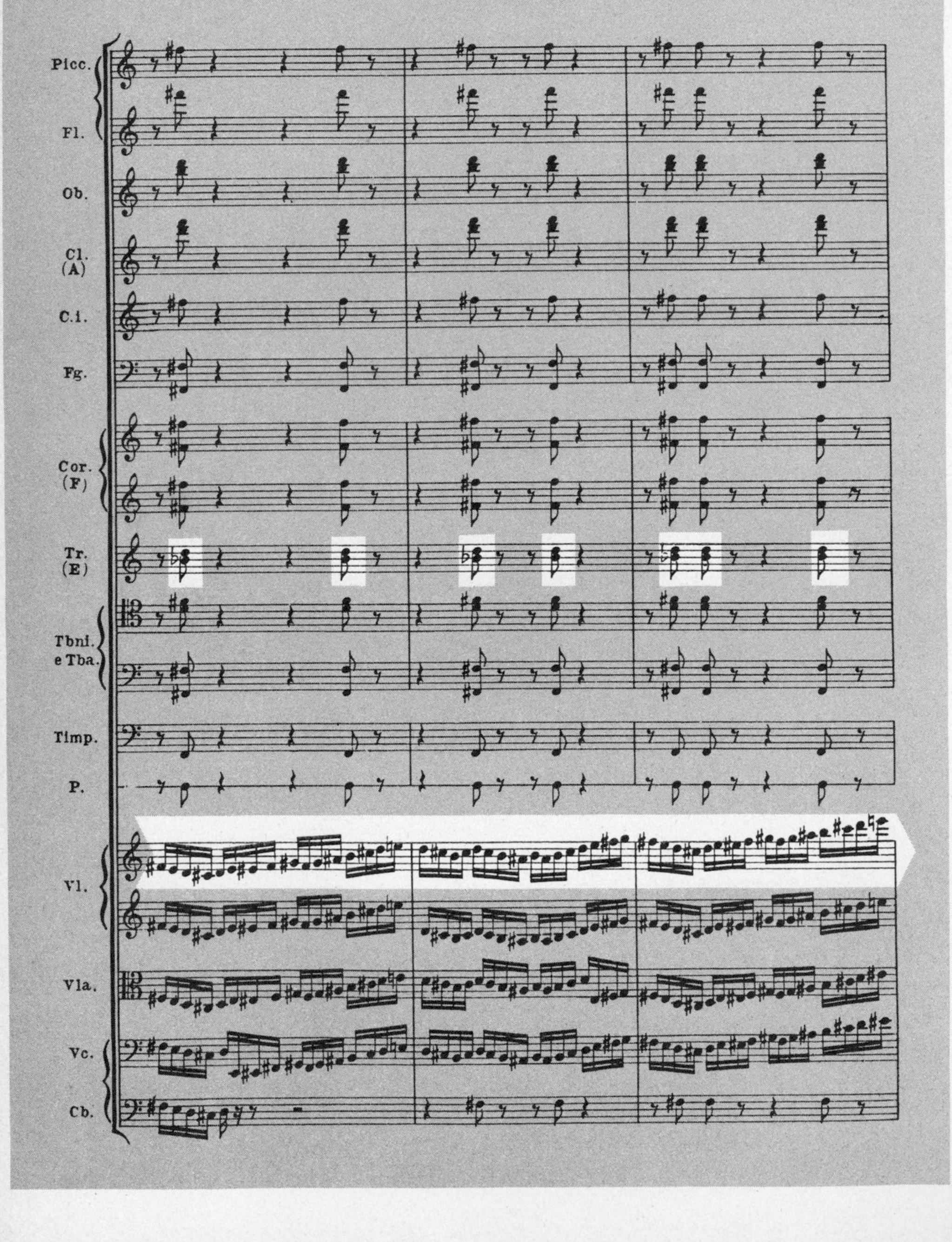
Picc.
Fl.
Ob.
Cl. (A)
C.i.
Fg.
Cor. (F)
Tr. (E)
Tbni. e Tba.
Timp.
P.
Vl.
Vla.
Vc.
Cb.

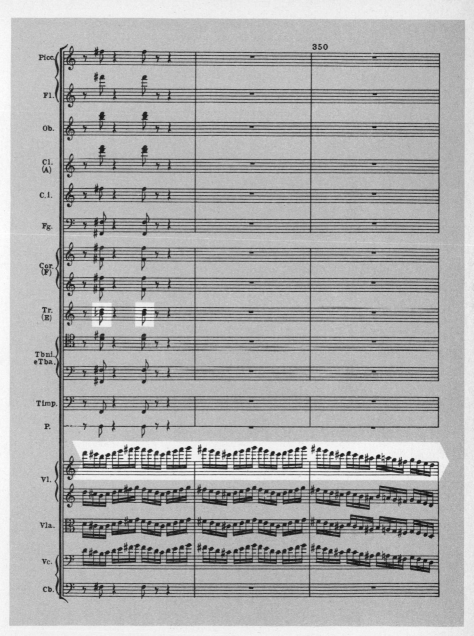

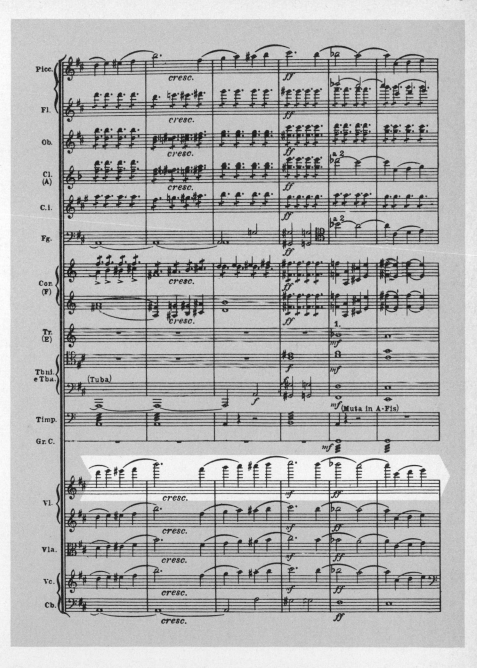

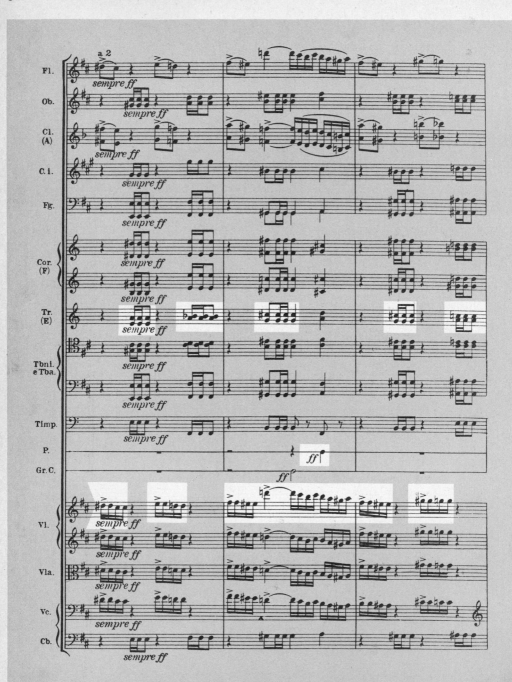

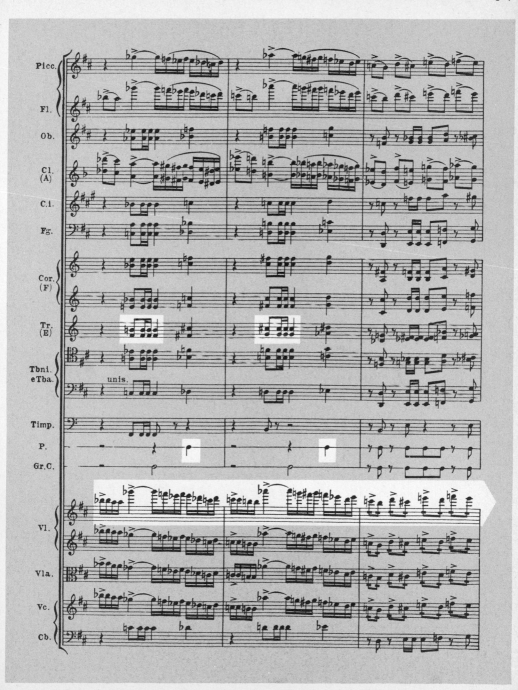

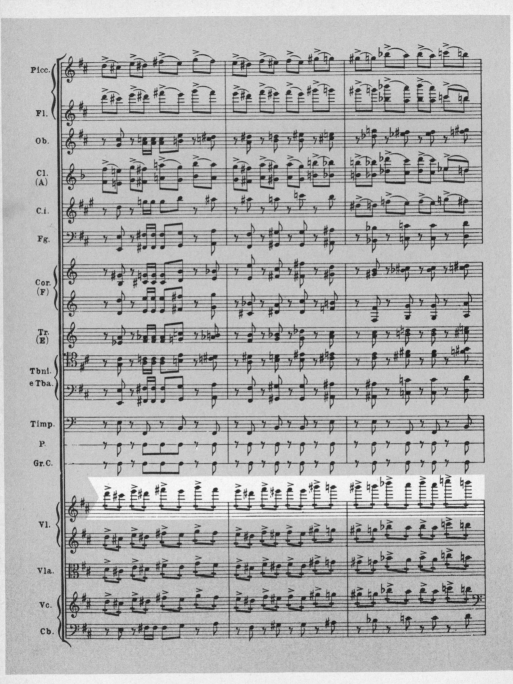

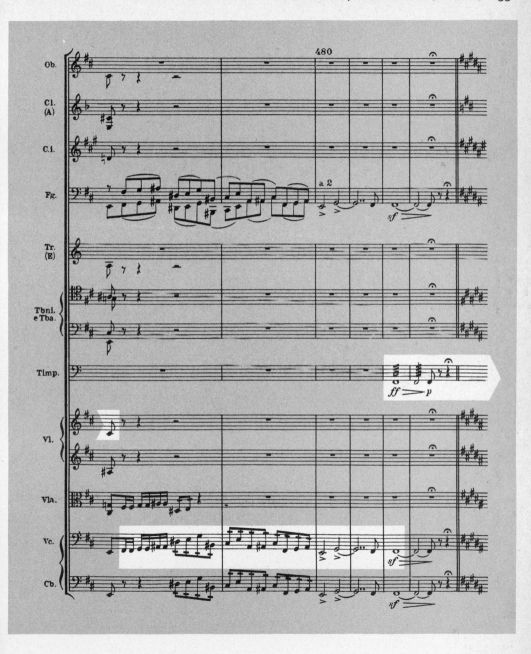

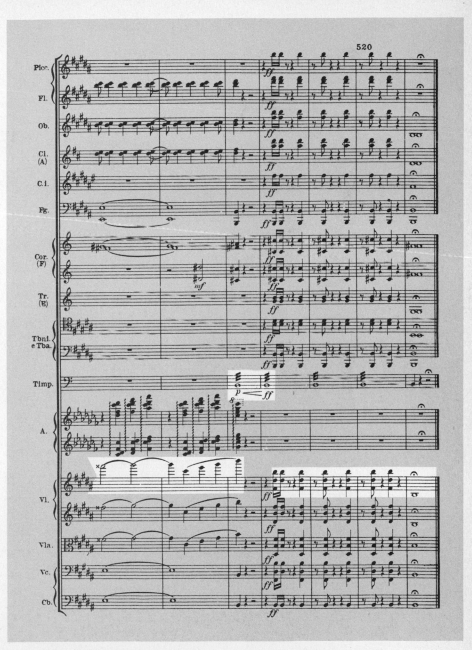

18. TCHAIKOVSKY, Excerpts from *The Nutcracker* (1892)
March

20
Fl.
Ob.
Cl.
Fg.
Cor.
(F)
Trbe.
(A)
Tbni.
Tuba
Piat.
Vl.
Vle.
Celli
C.-B.
mf
f
pizz.
arco

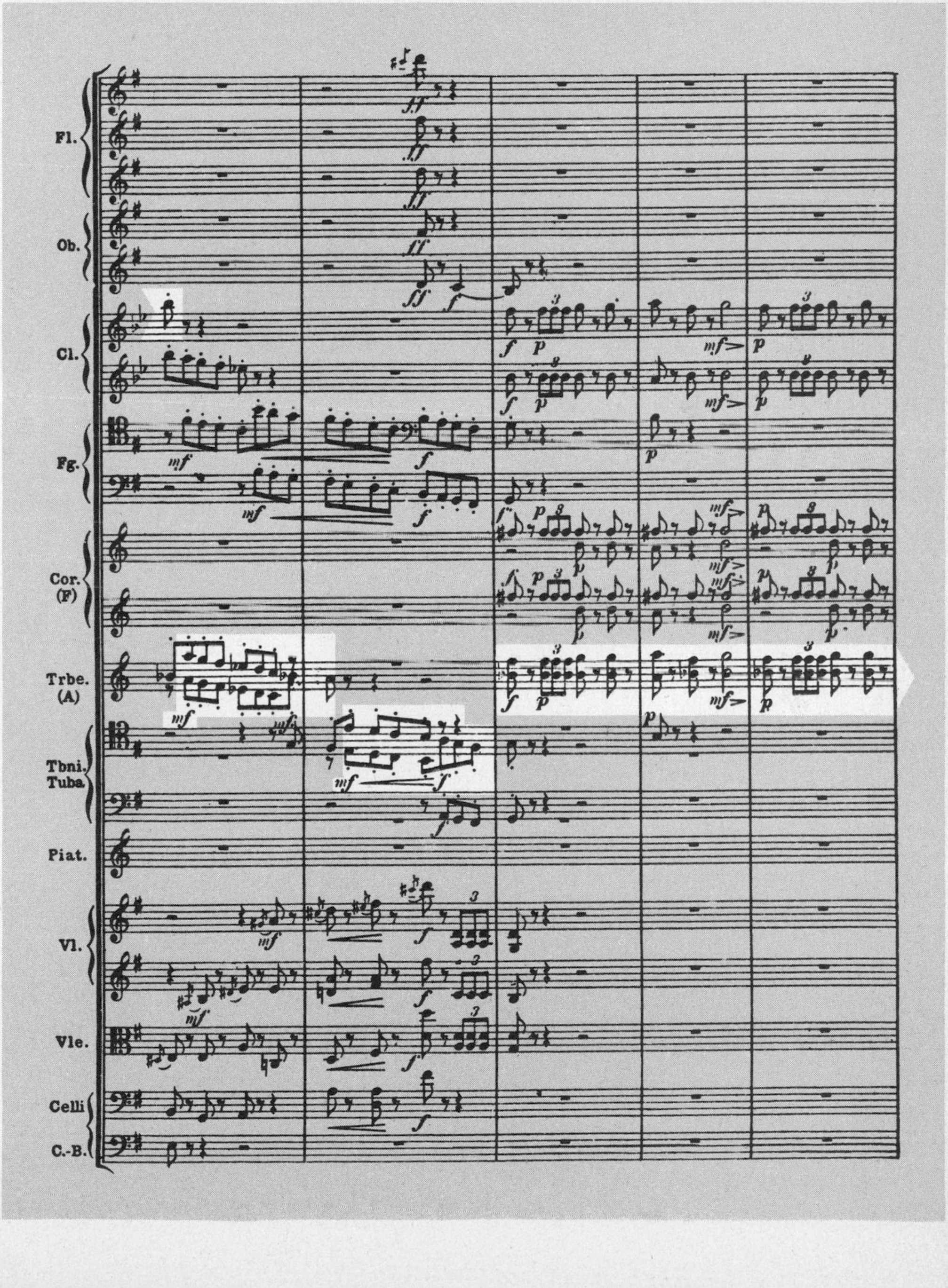
Fl.
Ob.
Cl.
Fg.
Cor. (F)
Trbe. (A)
Tbni. Tuba
Piat.
Vl.
Vle.
Celli
C.-B.

Fl.
Ob.
Cl.
Fg.
Cor. (F)
Trbe. (A)
Tbni. Tuba
Mit Paukenschlägel.
Piat.
Vl.
Vle.
Celli
C.-B.

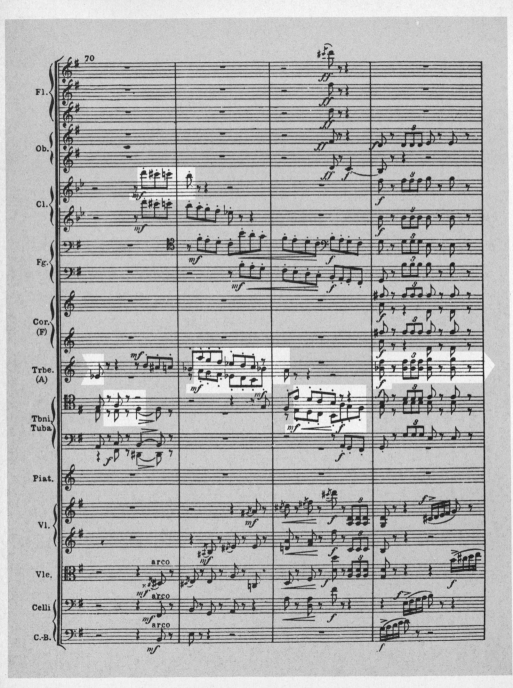

Arabian Dance

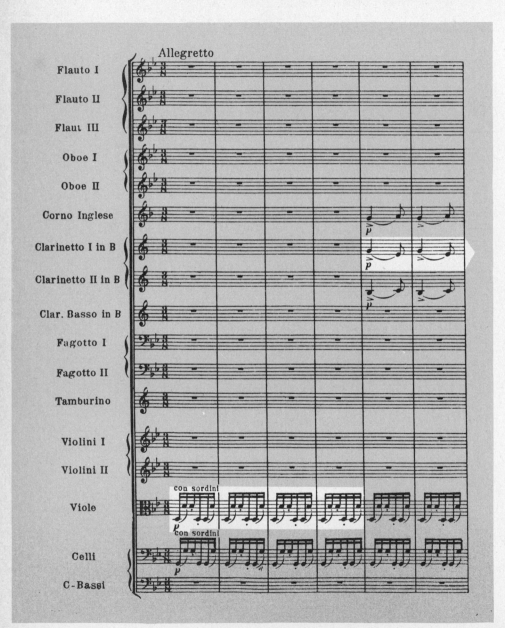

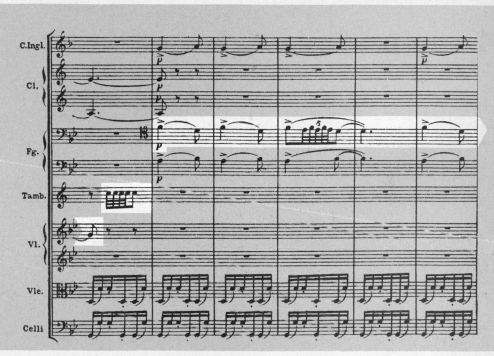

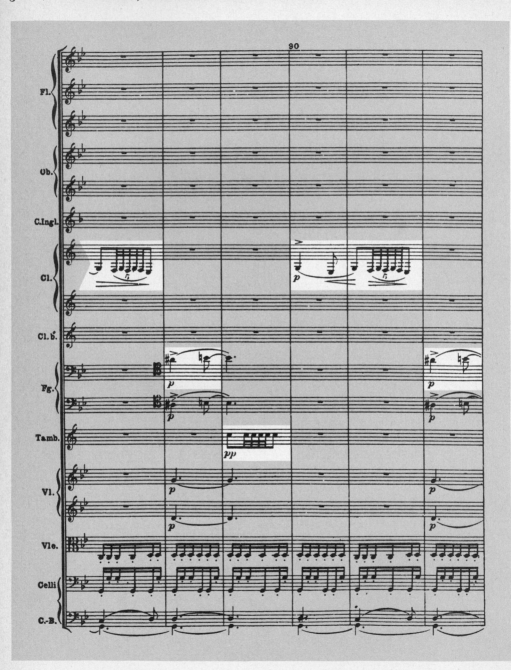

Dance of the Toy Flutes

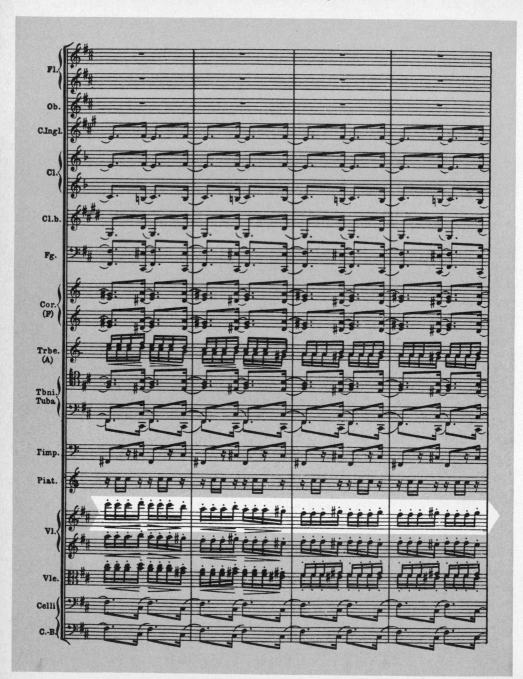

19. GIACOMO PUCCINI (1858-1924),
Scene from *La bohème*, Act I (1896)

Copyright, MCMLIV, by G. Schirmer, Inc.

Used by permission.

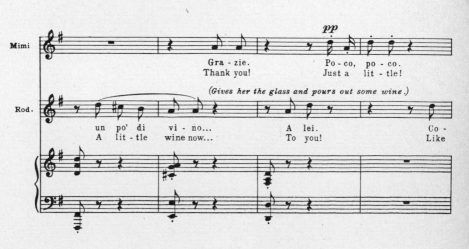

Andante lento ♩ = 40

Mimi: chia - ma - no Mi - mì, ma il mio no - me è Lu - ci - a.___
al - ways called Mi - mi, but my name is Lu - ci - a.___

Mimi: La sto - ria mia è bre - ve:___ A te - la o a se - ta ri - ca - mo in ca - sa e
My sto - ry is a brief one:___ I earn my liv - ing by sew - ing and em -

Mimi: fuo - ri... Son tran - quil - la e lie - ta ed è mio sva - go far gi - gli e
broi - der - ing. Work - ing gives me plea - sure; in lei - sure hours I make lil - ies and

Andante calmo ♩ = 54

Mimi: ro - se.___ Mi piac - cion quel - le co - se che han sì dol - ce ma -
ros - es.___ I dear - ly love those flow - ers, they de - light and en -

(36)

Allegretto moderato ♩ = 144

con semplicità

Mimi: So - la, mi fo il pran-zo da me stes - sa. Non va-do sem-pre a
Do - ing my work the day-time pass-es fair - ly, I go to Mass but

, *poco rall.* - - - - *a piacere*

Mimi: mes - sa ma pre-go as-sai il Si - gnor. Vi - vo so - la, so -
rare-ly, though ev -'ry night I pray. I live all by my -

a tempo

Mimi: let - ta, là in u - na bian - ca ca - me - ret - ta:
self. There from my loft - y gar - ret win - dow

poco rall. - - - -

Mimi: guar - do sui tet - ti e in cie - lo,
o - ver the roof-tops I see the sky.

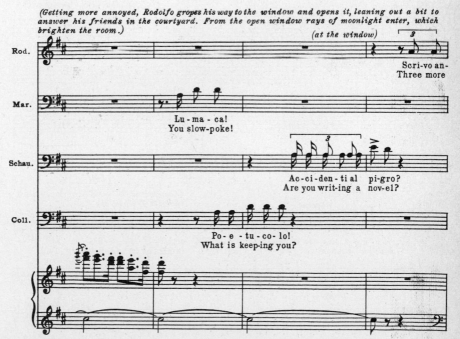

20. GUSTAV MAHLER (1860-1911),
Fourth movement from Symphony No. 4 (1900)

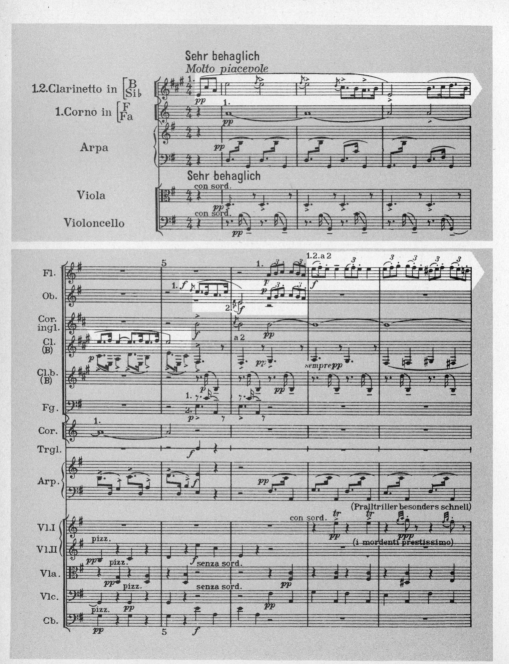

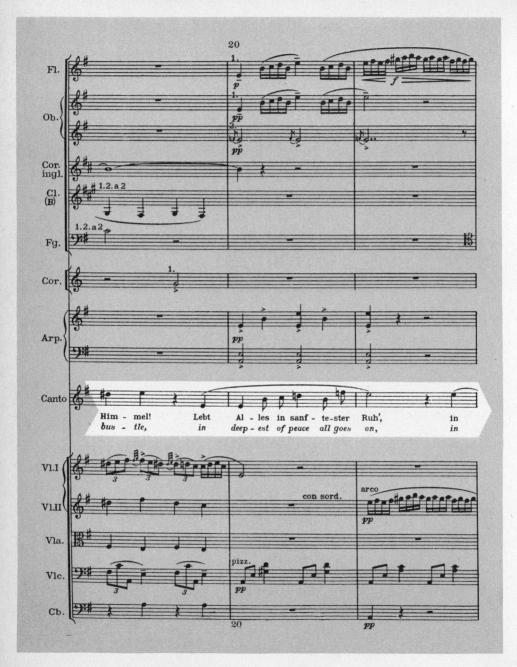

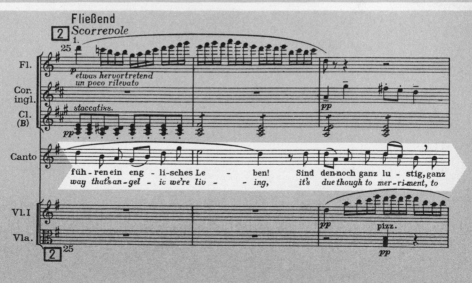

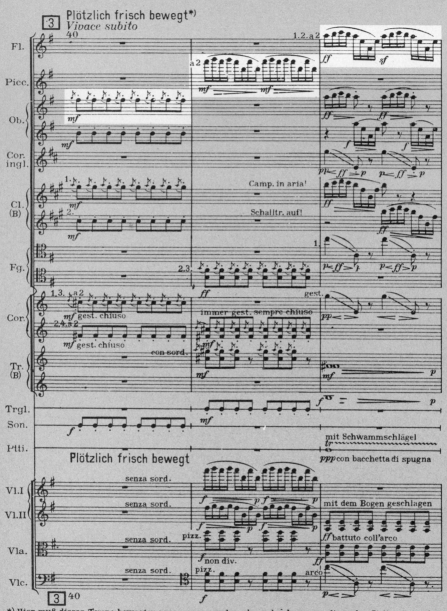

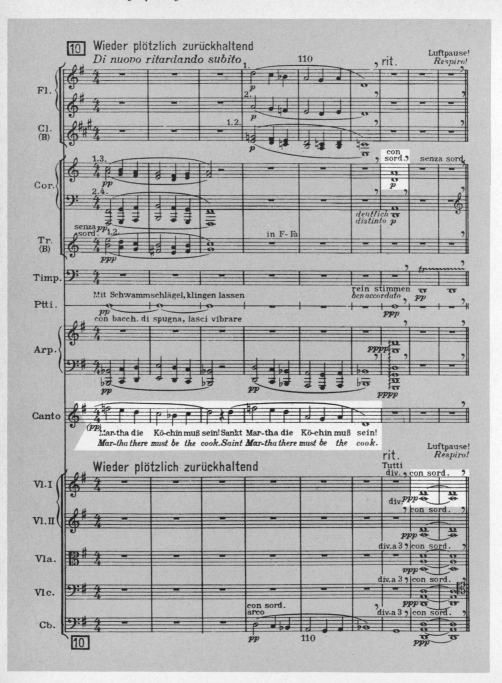

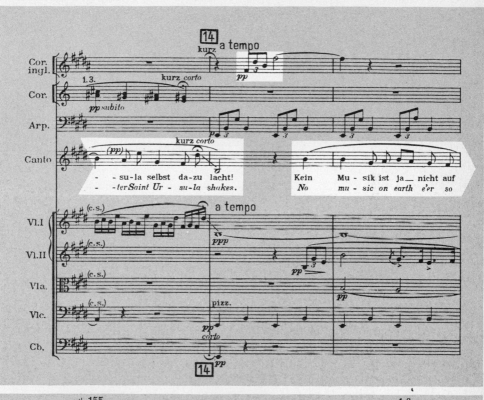

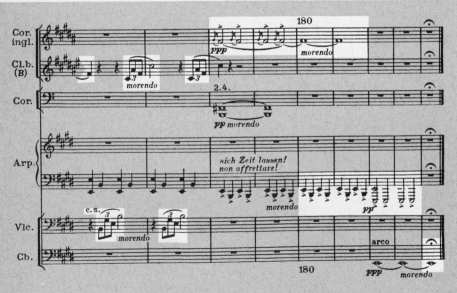

21. CLAUDE DEBUSSY (1862-1918),
Prelude to "The Afternoon of a Faun" (1894)

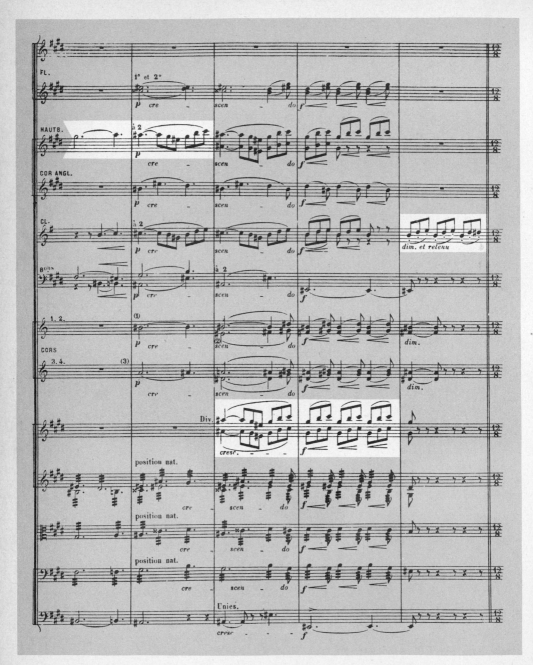

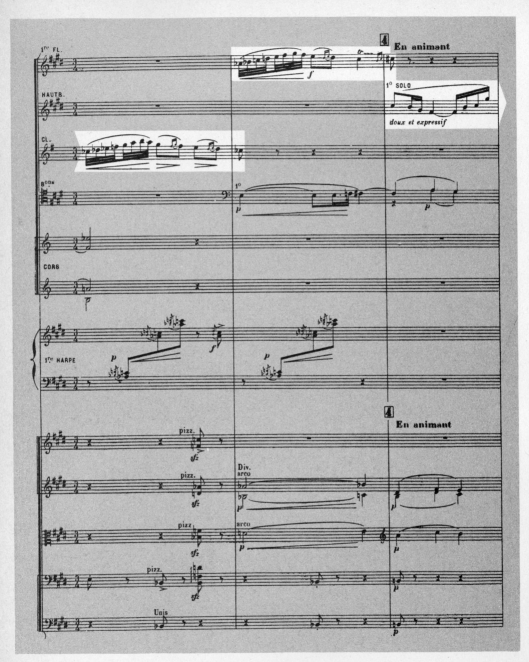

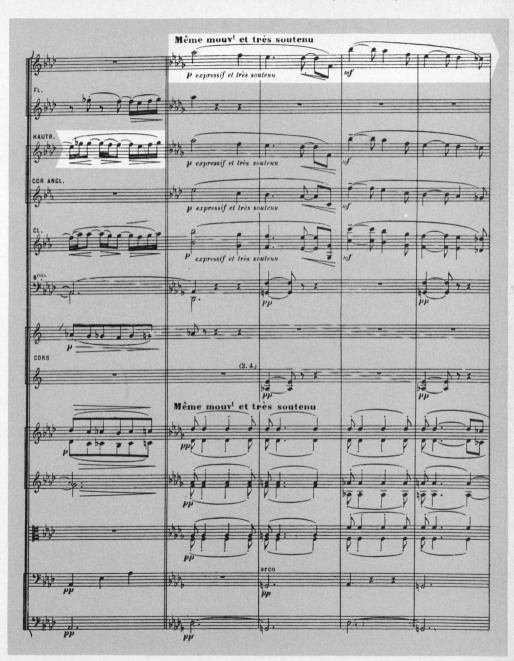

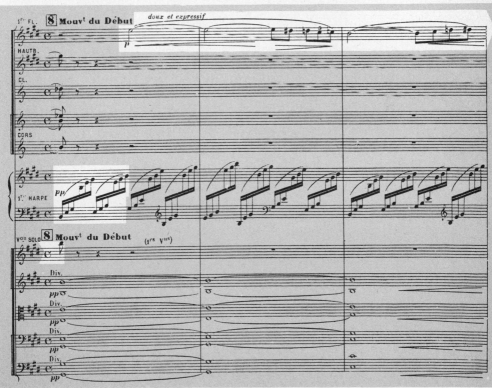

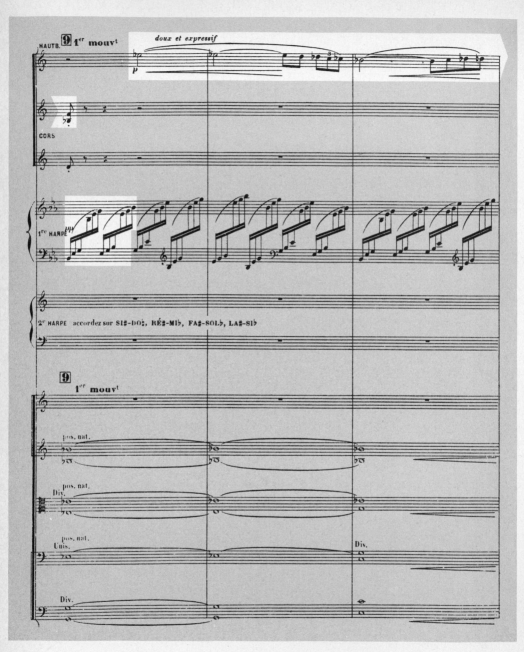

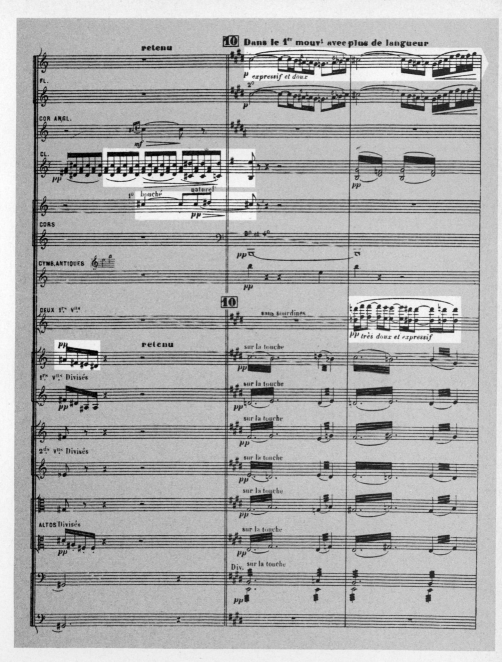

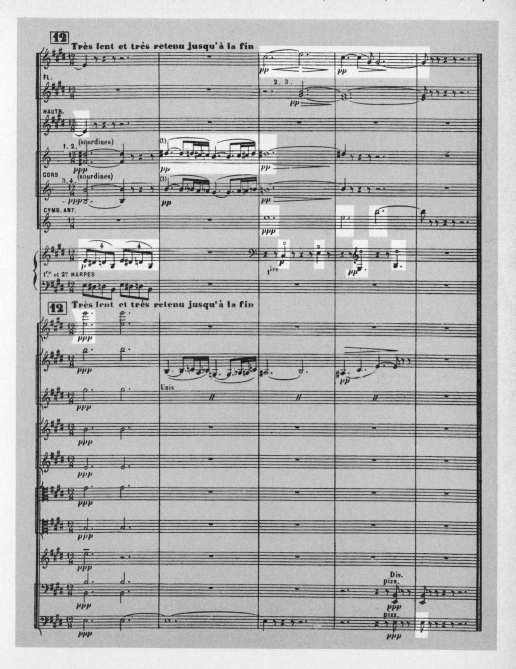

22. ARNOLD SCHOENBERG (1874-1951),
Excerpts from *FivePieces for Orchestra,* Opus 16 (1909, REV. 1949)
Vorgefühle

Nos. 1 and 2 from FIVE PIECES FOR ORCHESTRA, Opus 16, by Arnold Schoenberg, copyright ©
1952 by Henmar Press Inc., 373 Park Avenue South, New York, New York 10016. Reprinted with
permission of the publishers who publish the score of the complete work under Peters Edition
No. 6061.

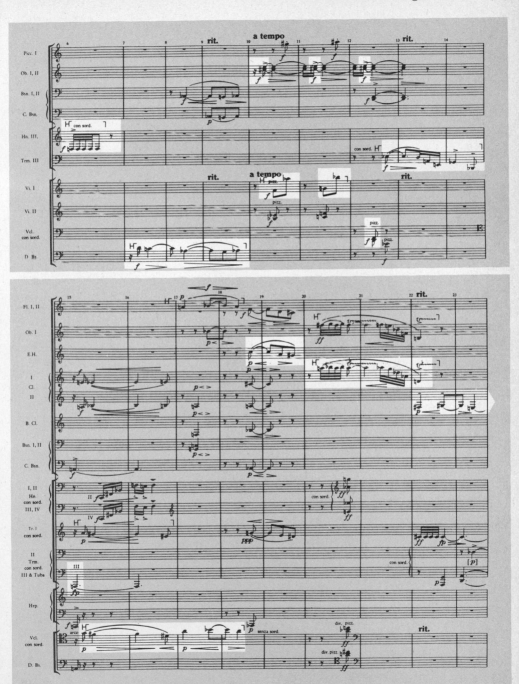

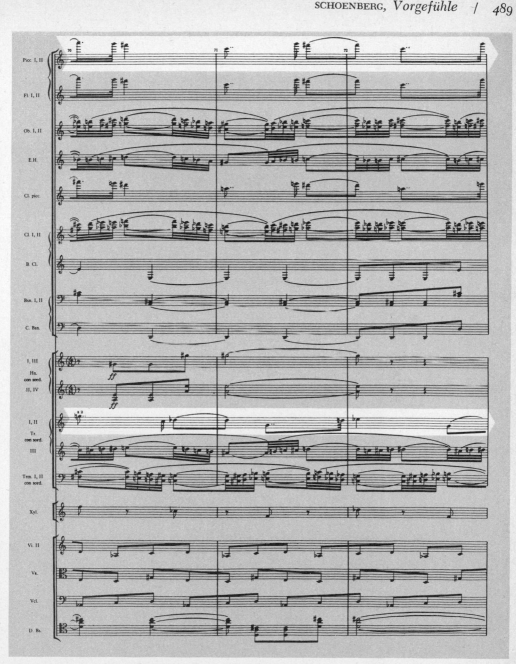

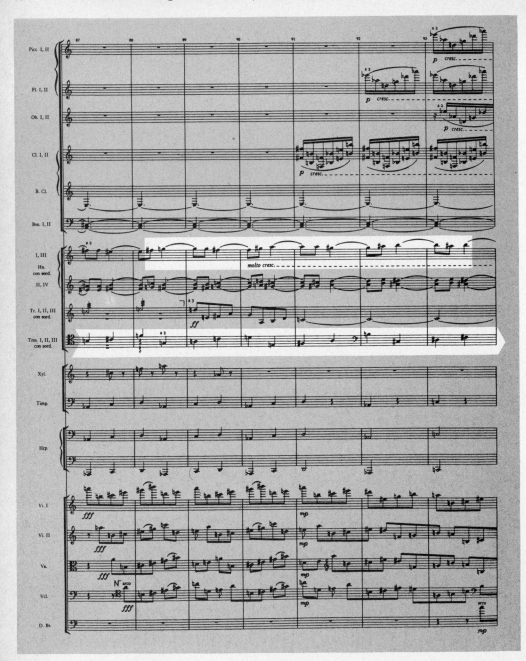

Vergangenes

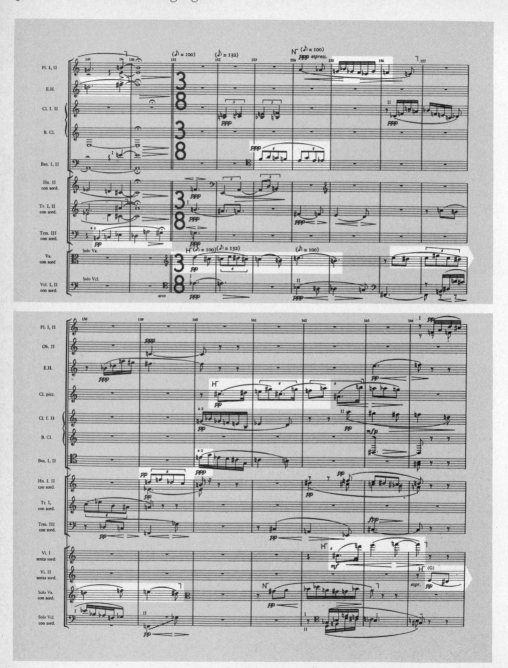

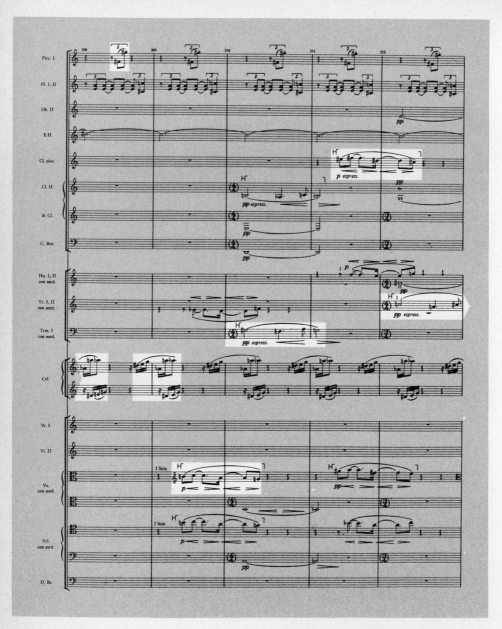

23. SCHOENBERG, *A Survivor from Warsaw* (1947)

PREFATORY NOTES

Our purpose in releasing a *revised edition* of Arnold Schoenberg's op. 46, "A Survivor from Warsaw" has been to publish a score that would not only reflect the composer's text but also attempt to solve the problems raised by any oversights contained therein. Thus, all proposed editorial suggestions and emendations have been placed between brackets, and the justification for these changes representing departures from the original text is offered below. To facilitate their listing, a table of the "set" with its transpositions and inversions has been adjoined, and coded in a succession of ordered groups as determined by the compositional unfolding. These sets have been notated in *well-tempered note-heads,* within the pitch-continuum's boundaries of their corresponding source-hexachords, in treble clef, and registered so as to minimize the need for ledger lines.

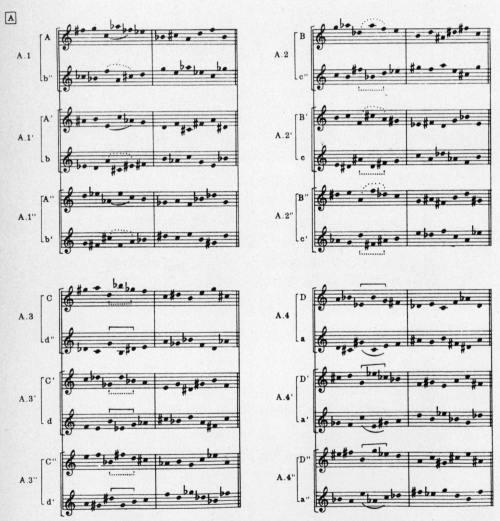

Reprinted by permission of the publisher, Boelke-Bomart, Inc., copyright 1949 by Bomart Music Publications. Revised Edition copyright 1974 by Boelke-Bomart, Inc. The Revised Edition is here included in its entirety at the request of the original publisher.

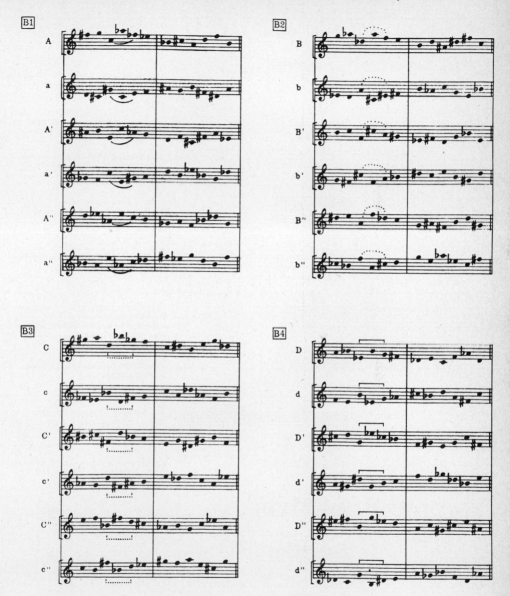

Bars	Beats	Instruments	Original text	Comments
5	4th	Harp	*(ff)*	Incomplete fourth beat in the manuscript short-score. Our revision cancels our first edition's amendment.
7	3rd	'Cello/Cbs.	*pp*	With [ʌ ʌ ʌ] in René Leibowitz' full-score transcript and the first edition.
13	3rd	Narrator	"most" also "much"	"Most" will be read in the short-score, Leibowitz' transcript, and the first edition; it is replaced by "much" on a separate typewritten text.
20-21		Viola Divisi	etc. *(pp)*	Amended in Leibowitz and the first edition.
22	4th ⅛th	Horns	*fp con sord.*	(4th horn — Eb) The second hexachord of "b" requires [E♮].
23	2nd	3 Violins Soli	*fp* con sord.	The fourth trichord of "A'" is missing. Amended on the basis of "A.1'", in the context of bars 22-23, and as part of the area 18-24. *See page VII.
31	1st-3rd	3 Violas Soli	*mf*	(A) ["C/Ab/Fb — F/A/C♯"] from "A.1" requires [Ab]. Amended in Leibowitz and our first edition.
32		Trumpet 1	*f*	Bar containing one beat too many. Our amendment maintains the obvious imitation between the horns and the trumpets.
33	3rd	Narrator	"Get out ! The	Beat containing one sixteenth-note too many. Amended in Leibowitz and the first edition.
34	3rd-4th	Violins I/II	*ff*	

As amended
in the first edition: *ff*

We are presently suggesting: *ff*

As amended
in the first edition: *ff*

We are presently suggesting: *ff*

As required by the first tetrad of "a", the order of the middle pitches, and suggested by motivic considerations.

Thus, from the upbeat to bar 34: the low strings and low brass unfold the first hexachords of "A" and "b'''" (A.1), and the upper woodwinds, upper strings and brass the first hexachords of "D" and "a" (A.4).

Bars	Beats	Instruments	Original text	Comments
35	3rd	Narrator	slowly	In a separately typewritten text.
40	4th	Narrator	*Stilljestanden!*	The spelling of the words in italics is Schoenberg's attempt to indicate a pronunciation corresponding to the Berlin dialect.
41	2nd	Narrator	o - der soll ich mit dem *Je -*	Beat containing one thirty-second-note too many. Amended in Leibowitz and the first edition.
43		Narrator	everybody	Amended in the first edition.
		Narrator	quiet or nervous	Amended in the first edition.
45	2nd-3rd	Trumpets 1, 2		Within bars 44-46, the progression "A.1" (A/<u>b</u>"), "A.1'" (A'/b), and "A.1''''"(A''/"<u>b</u>") requires F/F♯ as 3rd dyad of "<u>b</u>". Included in the first edition. *See page VII.
48	3rd	4th Horn		The 4th horn's entrance has been displaced from the 4th sixteenth of bar 49 to the 10th sixteenth of bar 48, thus replacing the 2nd horn from that point until the 1st sixteenth of bar 49
49	3rd	Narrator	floor	Amended in the first edition.
50	1st	Narrator	now	Amended in the first edition.
51				

51 A comparison between bar 11 and bar 51, particularly with respect to the intervallic relationships within and between both bars, as well as to similarities of registration (the specific inversion of the augmented triad in bar 11 is stated in the flutes in bar 10; the relationship of the viola E-C in bar 50 to the augmented triad of bar 51 is analogous), provides the basis for our amendment. The manuscript reads C/E/Ab for the first three beats and most of the fourth. Schoenerg then corrected the fourth beat for E/Ab/C. It appears to be an incomplete correction.

Bars	Beats	Instruments	Original text	Comments
54	4th	Narrator	know	Revised amendment.
66	1st	Viola/'Cello	*p* pizz.	The 3rd trichord of "b'''" requires a [C♮]; C♯ (D♭) belongs to the 2nd dyad of the first hexachord and is scored for both trumpets.
66	2nd-4th	Piccolos 1, 2	*ff*	The last three beats of this bar state the combinatorial pair of first hexachords of "A.1''''"; "b'''"is scored for the lower strings, and "A''''" for the remaining instruments. In this context, the dyad scored for the piccolos should be [G/F♯] and not E/D♯.

The 2nd beat of bar 72 begins a progression, in three asymmetric sections, unfolding all combinatorial pairs of first hexachords A. Each hexachord is set in opposite registers, so that when the relationship between combinatorial pairs is inverted, the linear succession of content hexachords is maintained. The first section sets the following words: *"one, two, three, four, became faster, and faster, so fast that it finally sounded like a stampede of wild horses,"* by

"A.1"$\frac{b''|A}{A|b''}$; "A.2"$\frac{c''|B}{B|c''}$; "A.3"$\frac{d''|C}{C|d''}$; "A.4"$\frac{a|D}{D|a}$; the second section: *"and all of a sudden, in the middle of it*

they began singing by "A.1'"$\frac{b|A'}{A'|b}$; "A.2'"$\frac{c|B'}{B'|c}$; "A.3'"$\frac{d|C'}{C'|d}$; and "A.4'"$\frac{a'|D'}{D'|a'}$ and the third section:

"the *SCHeMA"* by "A.1''''"$\frac{b'|A''}{A''|b'}$; and "*YISROeL"* by "A.2''''"$\frac{c'|B''}{B''|c'}$ "A.4''''". the last, "A.3''''"$\frac{a''}{C''|d'|D''}$

a unique grouping of hexachordal associations, which is compositionally the culmination of the progression, and the articulation for the setting of the prayer SCHeMA YISROeL. Against this background, a number of pitches become problematical, and two are missing. It should be mentioned that the multiplication of each possible error has its origin in the instrumental doublings in the full score transcript.

Bars	Beats	Instruments	Original text	Comments
71	2nd-3rd	Narrator	began	The relationship between the beginning of this paragraph and that of the preceding one suggests "They [started] again"; however, the rhythmic associations within the rhythmic setting of the text, as well as those between the set text and the music do not suggest a satisfactory solution.
73	3rd-4th	Cl. 2/Bsn. 1 Hrp. Violins I/II		The first dyad of "A" requires F♯/G.
74	1st-3rd	Cl.2/Bsn. 1 Harp. Violins I/II		The second trichord of "c⁗" requires (C/B/F♯)/[B♭]/D/[E♭].

It will be observed that the *two missing pitches* — B♭ and E♭ from "c⁗" — are first presented in this edition in their inverse order. Contextually, this was suggested by the fact that the trichordal partitioning of both A/b″ (A.1) — bars 72-73 — as well as B/c″ (A.2) — bars 74-75 — contain at least one retrograde of a second trichord of each pair in question, this in contrast to the exclusively onward statement of all trichords found in "A.3", the end of the progression's first section. The improbability of the triple reiteration of the woodwind/harp dyad B/F♯ (G. 74), or the alternative, a single reiteration of tetrad B/F♯ /B♭ and E♭ (b. 74) creating an awkward motivic association with the beginning (b. 72) that is quite out of context, as well as the local points of attack of the pitches scored for the violins I/II tend to confirm the validity of our amendment. The reiteration associated with the entry of each hexachord pair is subjected to variation, compression and ultimate dissolution by bar 80. Underlying these developments are successive transformations of metrical groupings: 4 beats+3 beats within 7, 3+2 within 5, 3+3 within 6, 2+2 overlapping 1½, etc. The metrical contraction culminates at the point of greatest hexachordal density, (b. 80) "YISROᵉL." This result in a nonsequential statement of sequential material.

Bars	Beats	Instruments	Original text	Comments
75	2nd-4th	Cl.2/Bsn.1 Harp. Violins I/II		The second trichord of "d⁗" requires B/E♭/[E].
76	1st-3rd	Cl.2/Bsn. 1 Harp. Violins I/II		The second trichord of "C" requires [B♭]/F♯/F.
77	4th	Narrator	quite	Amended in the first edition.
78	2nd-3rd	Fl.1, 2 Ob. 1, 2 Cl. 1, 2 Horns 3, 4		The first hexachord of "c" requires E/[D♯]/B♭/D/[F♯]/G.
80	1st-2nd	Ob. 1, 2 Cl. 1, 2		The first dyad of "B⁗" requires [E♭]/E.

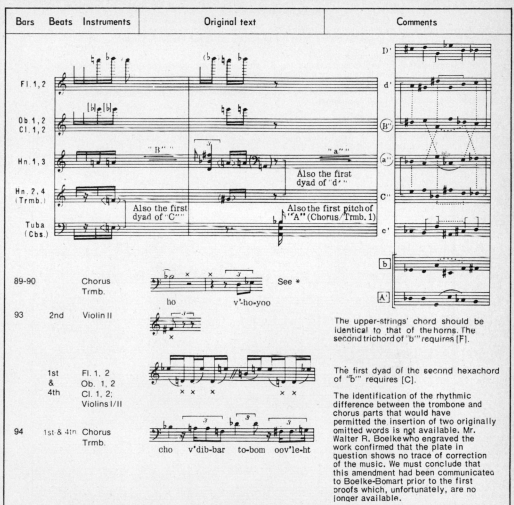

Bars	Beats	Instruments	Original text	Comments

89-90 Chorus, Trmb. — ho / v'-ho-yoo — See *

93 2nd Violin II — The upper-strings' chord should be identical to that of the horns. The second trichord of "b'" requires [F].

1st & 4th Fl. 1, 2; Ob. 1, 2; Cl. 1, 2; Violins I/II — The first dyad of the second hexachord of "b'" requires [C].

94 1st & 4th Chorus, Trmb. — cho v'dib-bar to-bom oov'le-ht — The identification of the rhythmic difference between the trombone and chorus parts that would have permitted the insertion of two originally omitted words is not available. Mr. Walter R. Boelke who engraved the work confirmed that the plate in question shows no trace of correction of the music. We must conclude that this amendment had been communicated to Boelke-Bomart prior to the first proofs which, unfortunately, are no longer available.

55-96 page 24 R. Leibowitz—4th line: a; 22nd line: tranquille; 26th line: malgre; 31st line: mi-conscient; 37th line: wie viele; M. Peter—5th line: lassigte; 24th line: helfen?; 38th line: Eins; 41st line: wie viele; last line: SCHeMAISRAeL

(The double octaves, between the 1st clarinet and 4th horn (F/F), and between the 2nd clarinet and 'cello (F♯/F♯) in bar 55, the triple octave between the flutes/violins I/II and the 1st bassoon/2nd trombone/'cello (C/C), the double octave between the upper horns and the tuba/contrabass (A/A) in bar 80, the octave between the 2nd trumpet/violin II and 1st trombone (E♭/E♭) in bar 86, and the octave between the trumpet/violin II and 1st trombone (E♭/E♭) in bar 86, and the octave between the 1st and 2nd trombones (C/C) in bar 96 are Schoenberg's and no amendment is necessary.)

*These amendments also duplicate three amongst a number of black pencilled insertions—probably in the composer's handwriting—incorporated into the blue-print copy of Renè Leibowitz' full-score transcript included by Schoenberg in the documentation submitted for the first edition. The latter sets two originally omitted words. None of these amendments, as well as that of bar 94 has been transferred to the manuscript short-score. "A Survivor from Warsaw" was written between the 11th and 23rd of August 1947. Schoenberg's manuscript short-score and Renè Leibowitz' full-score transcript (Hollywood—December 1947) are at the Library of Congress (Koussevitzky Foundation), Washington, D.C.

I gratefully acknowledge the interest, generosity and assistance of Mrs. Lilo Gladir, Professor Claudio Spies and Mr. Thomas James.

Jacques-Louis Monod — New York 1973

EXPLANATORY NOTES

Principal parts are marked at their beginning P, at their ending ⅂. They must not be played louder than indicated. Parts not marked P, must be played in such a manner that the important parts can easily dominate.

There are three kinds of detached notes:
  1) notes which are not so long as legato notes, i.e. not shortened but only separated from the next notes.
  2) staccato, marked ˈ are notes similar to martellato notes, short, heavy, accented, hard.
  3) spiccato, marked • are short, but light, elastic notes.
  The metronome‑marks need not be taken literally—primarily they should give a fair idea of the tempo in respect to the character of each section in all its changes.

Col legno tratto means "drawn with the bow stick." *Col legno battuto* means "tapped with the bow stick." *Ponticello, sul ponticello.* It is not sufficient to play "near the bridge." In order to produce the "immaterial sonority" desired here, the bow (or if *col legno*, the bow stick) must actually touch the bridge.

A. Schoenberg

The score is notated in C

° "Count off!"

° "Attention!"
°° "Quicker! Start again from the beginning. In a minute I will
know how many I will send to the gas chamber; Count off!"

The narrator text reads:
They [be-gan] a-gain, first slow-ly: one — two — three — four, became fast-er and

fast-er; so fast that it finally sounded like a stampede of wild horses,

Translation

Sh^ema Yisroel Adonoy elohenoo Adonoy ehod | Hear, O Israel, the Lord is our God, the Lord is one.

V^eohavto es Adonoy eloheho b^ehol l^evov^eho oov^ehol nafsh^eho [oov^ehol m^eodeho] | You shall love the Lord your God with all your heart and with all your soul [and with all your might].

V^ehoyoo hadd^evoreem hoelleh asher onohee m^etsavv^eho hayyom al l^evoveho | And these words which I command you today shall be in your heart.

V^eshinnantom l^evoneho v^edibbarto bom [b^eshivt^eho b^eveteho] oov^eleht^eho baddereh oov^eshohb^eho oov^ekoomeho. | You shall teach them diligently to your children, and you shall speak of them [when you are sitting at home and] when you go on a journey.

24. CHARLES IVES (1874-1954), *Putnam's Camp, Redding, Connecticut*, from *Three Places in New England* (1903-1914)

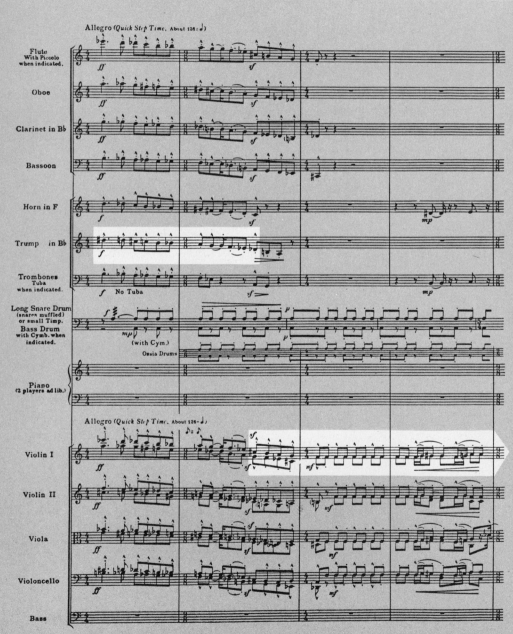

Copyright 1935, Mercury Music Corporation. Used by permission.

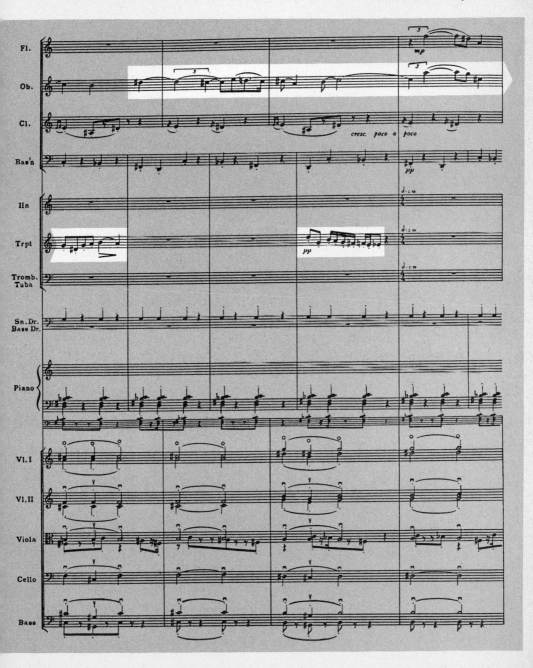

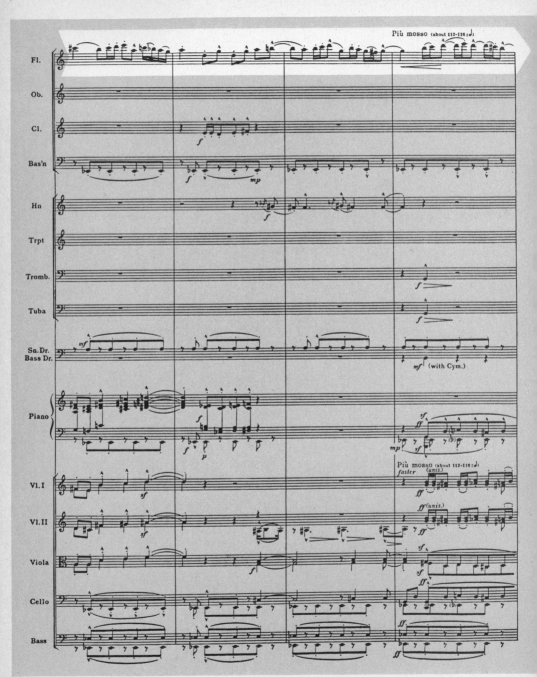

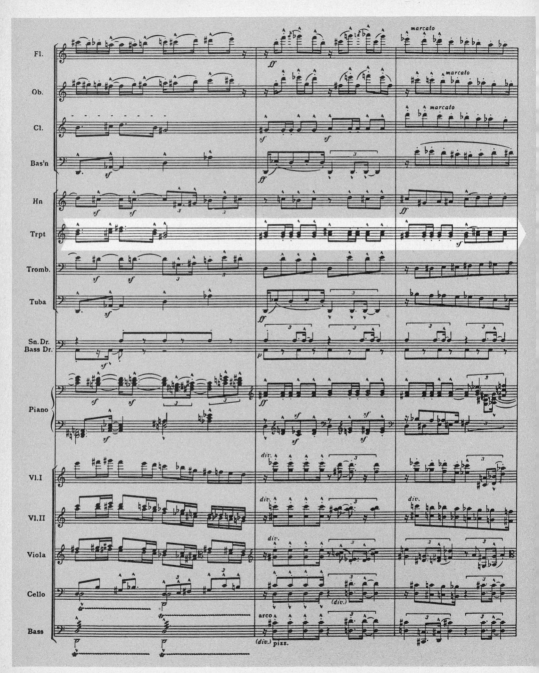

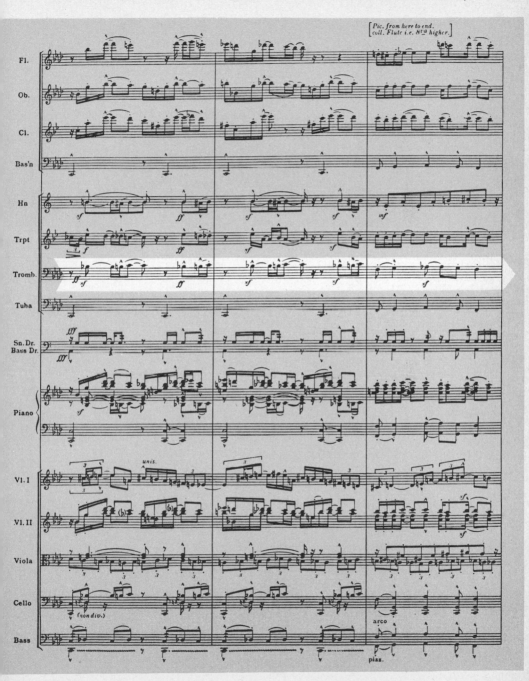

25. BÉLA BARTÓK (1881-1945), First movement from
Music for Strings, Percussion, and Celesta (1936)

Copyright 1937 by Universal Edition; Renewed 1964. Copyright and Renewal Assigned to Boosey & Hawkes, Inc. for the U.S.A. Reprinted by permission.

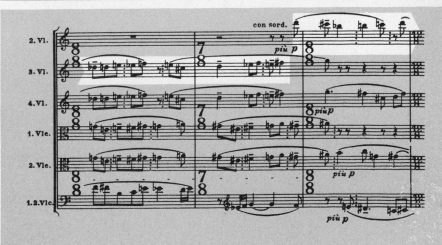

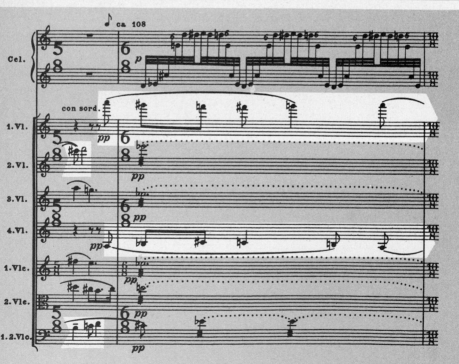

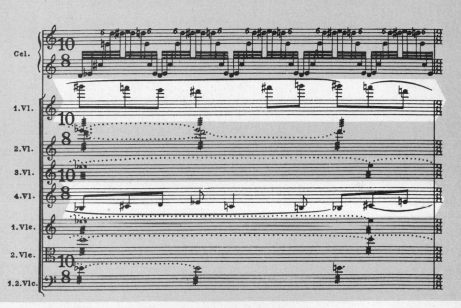

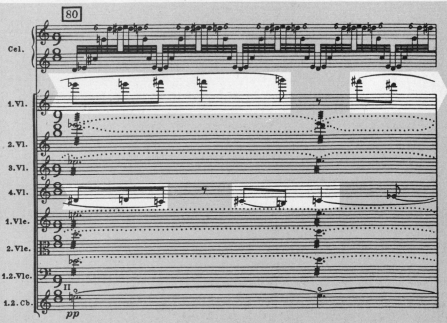

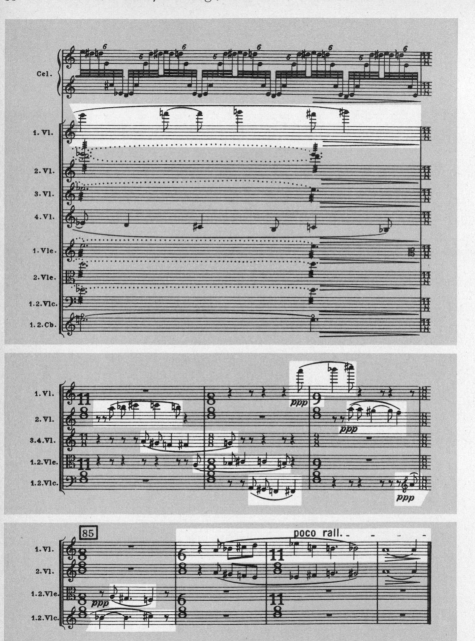

26. IGOR STRAVINSKY (1882-1971), Excerpts from *The Rite of Spring* (1913)

Opening scene

Rite of Spring, Igor Stravinsky. Copyright 1921 by Edition Russe de Musique. Copyright assigned 1947 to Boosey & Hawkes, Inc. Reprinted by permission of Boosey & Hawkes, Inc., and Boosey & Hawkes (Canada) Ltd.

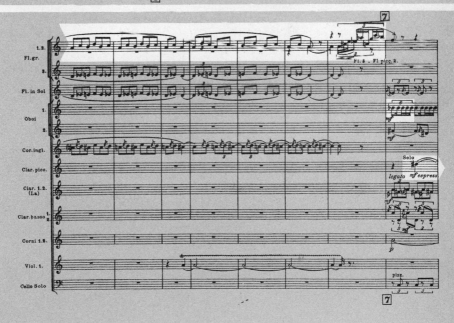

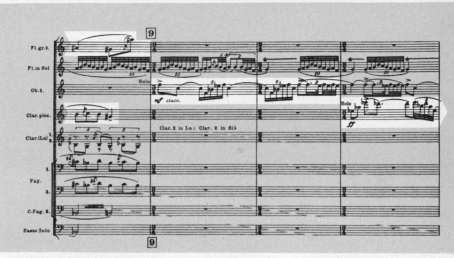

Augurs of Spring — Dances of the Youths and Maidens

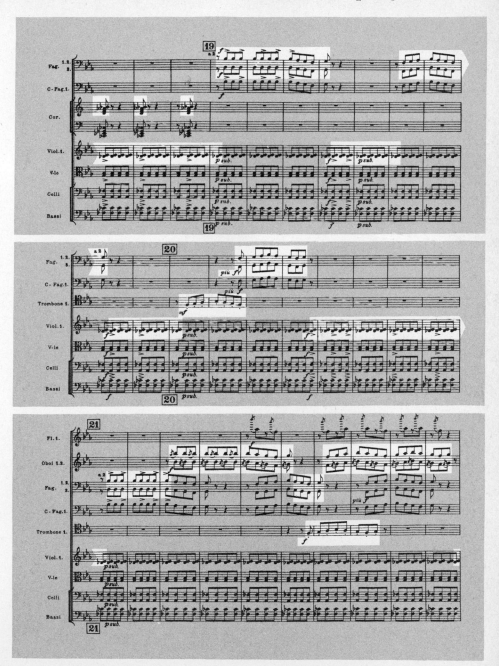

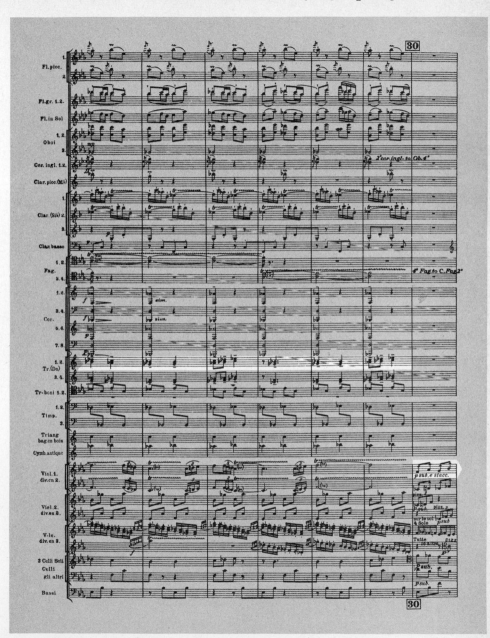

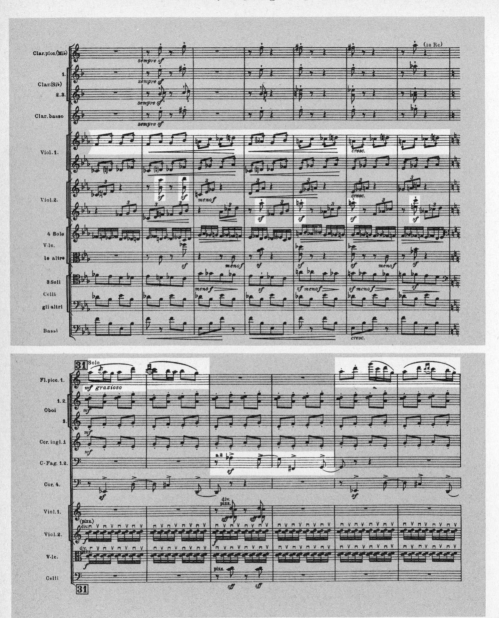

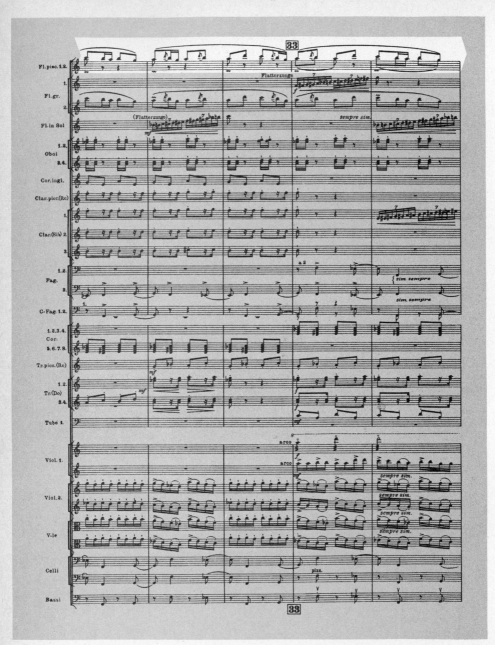

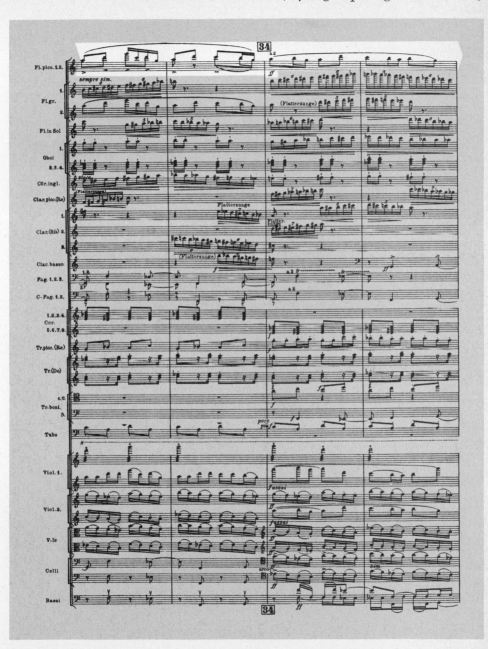

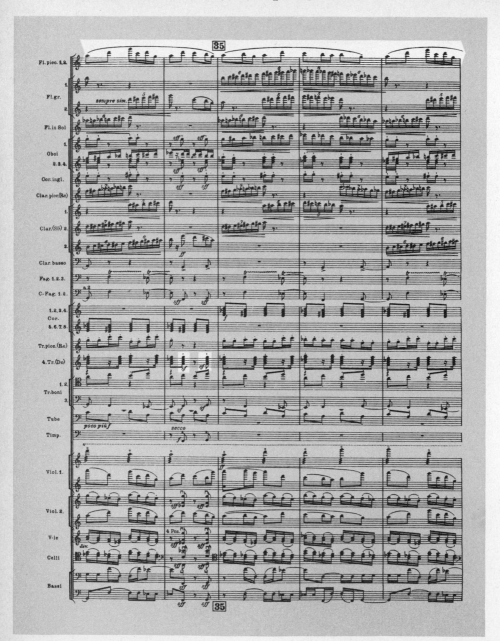

Ritual of Abduction

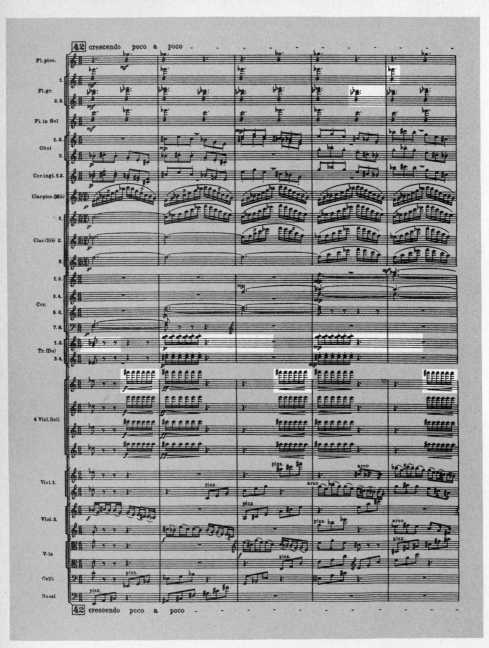

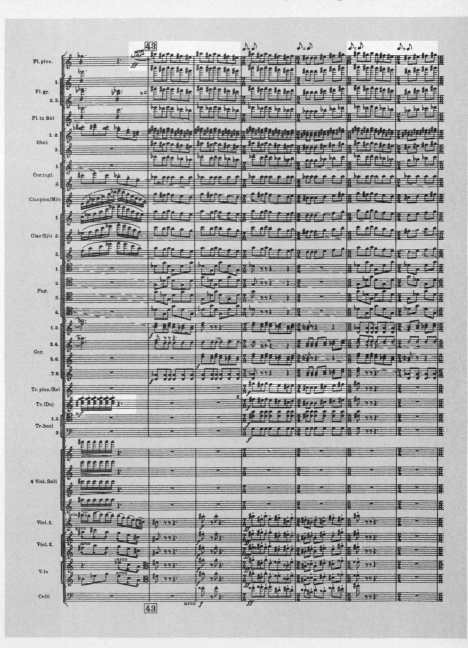

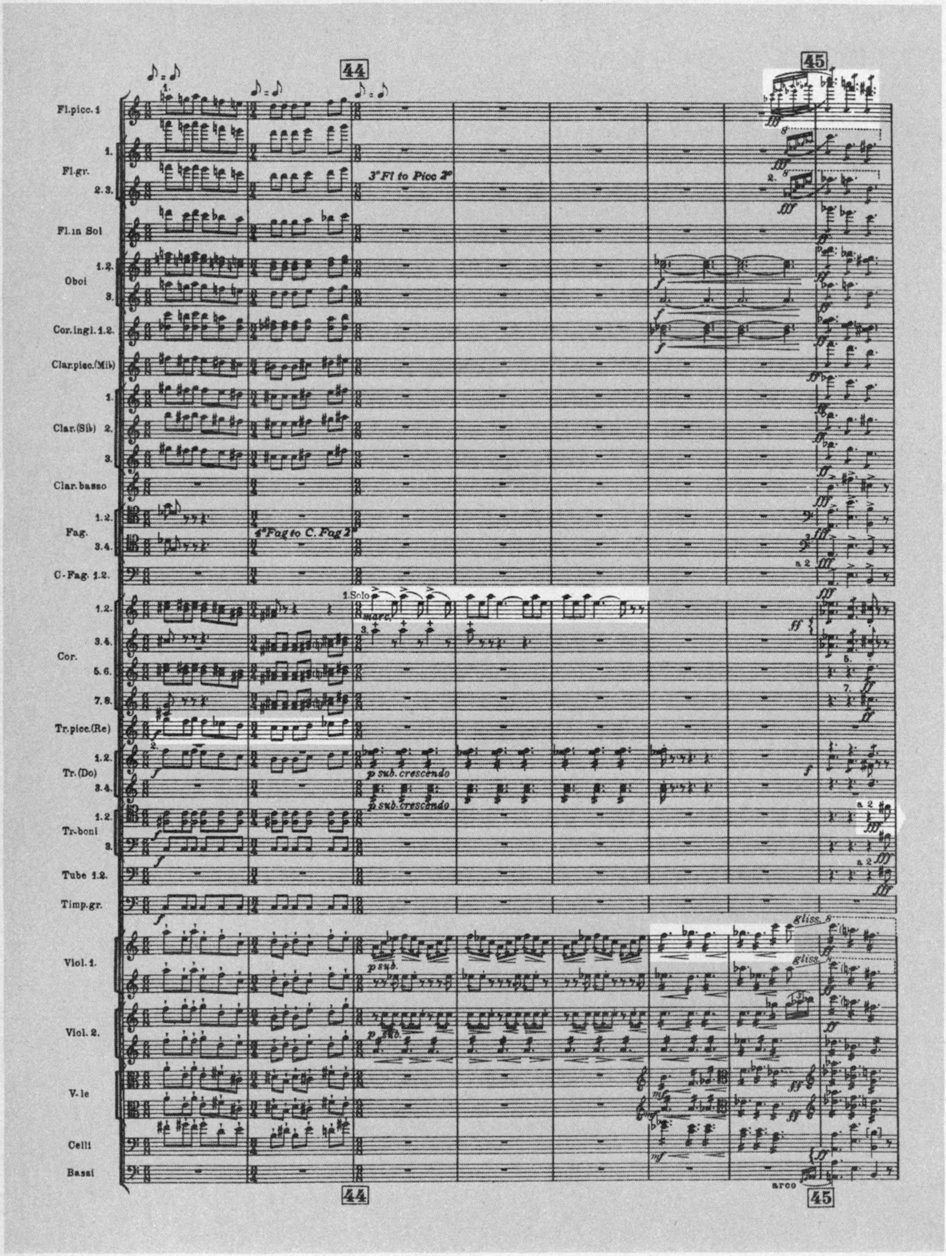
44
45
Fl.picc. 1
Fl.gr.
3° Fl to Picc 2°
Fl. in Sol
Oboi
Cor. ingl. 1.2.
Clar.picc.(Mib)
Clar.(Sib)
Clar. basso
Fag.
4° Fag to C. Fag 2°
C-Fag. 1.2.
1. Solo
marc.
Cor.
Tr.picc.(Re)
Tr.(Do)
p sub. crescendo
Tr-boni
a 2
Tube 1.2.
Timp.gr.
Viol. 1.
p sub.
gliss.
Viol. 2.
V-le
Celli
Bassi
arco

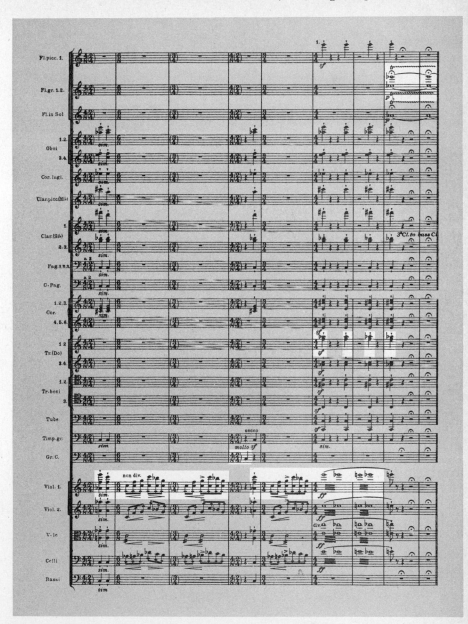

Danse sacrale

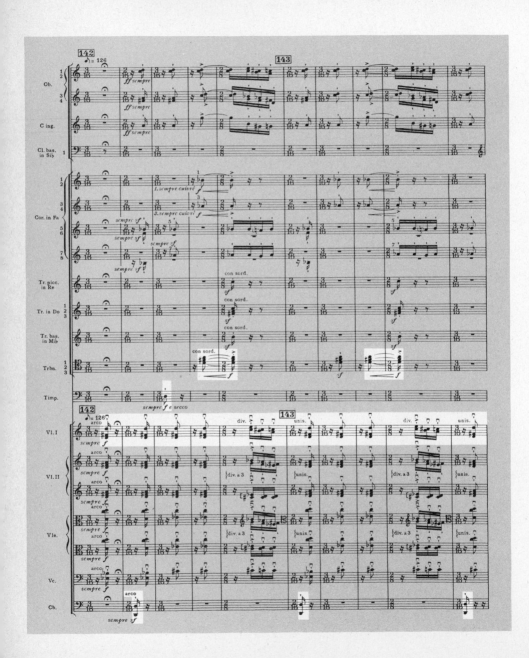

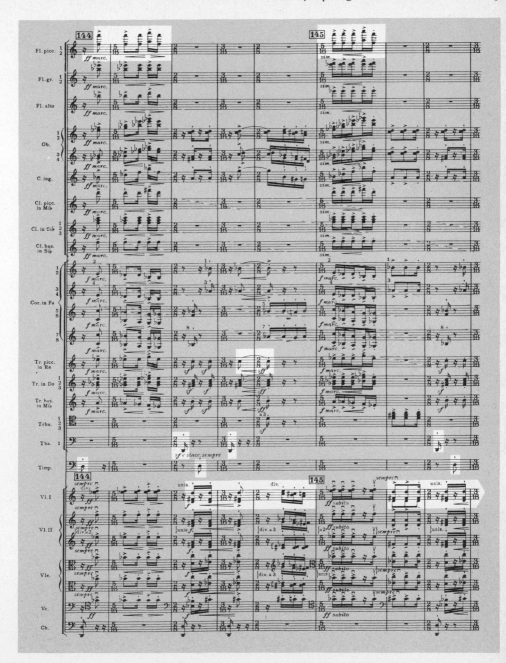

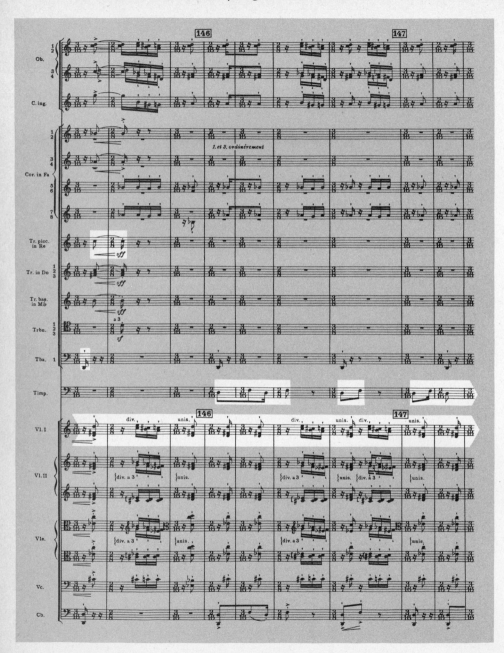

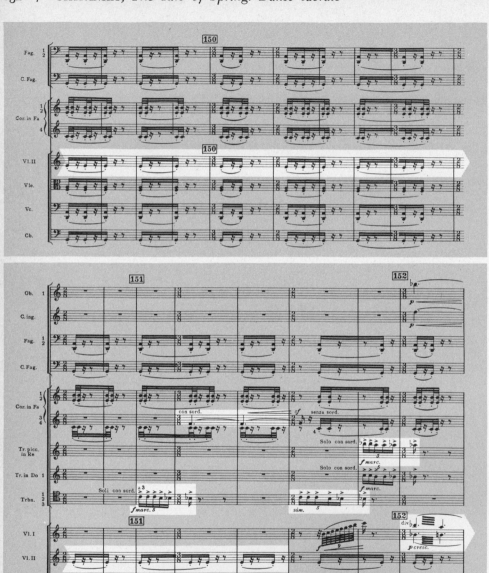

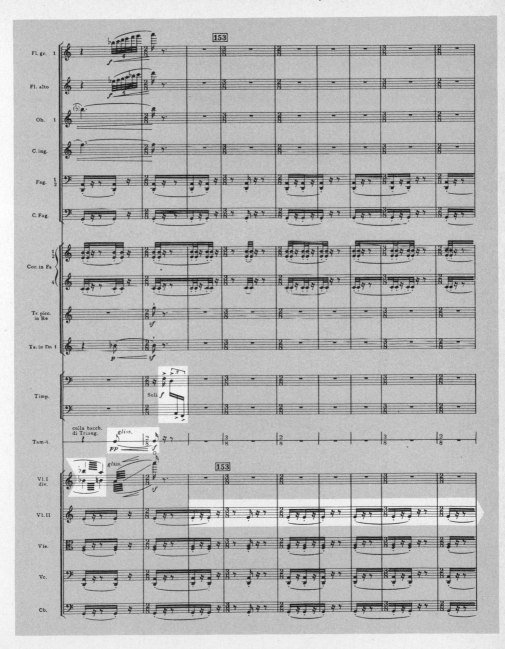

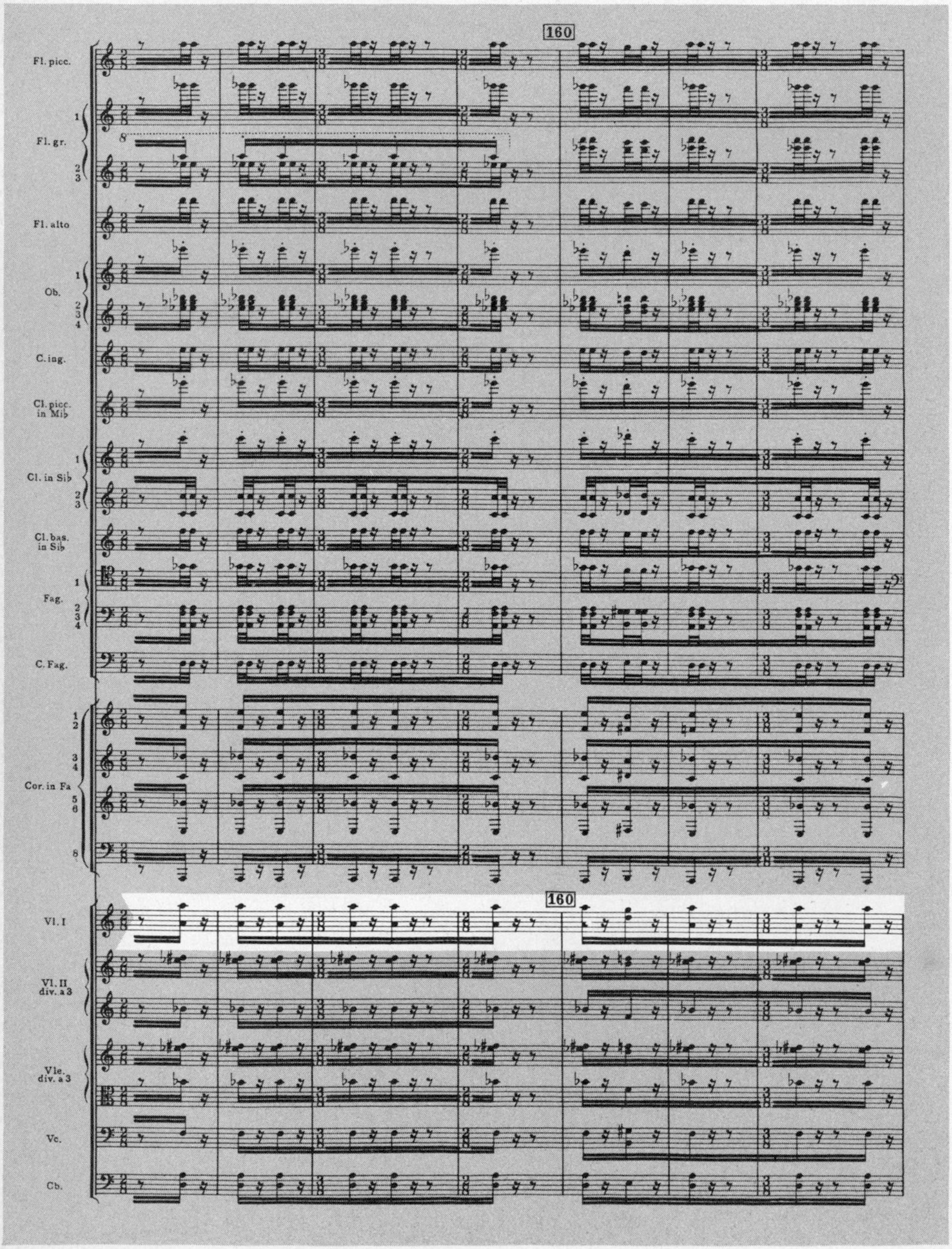
160
Fl. picc.
Fl. gr.
Fl. alto
Ob.
C. ing.
Cl. picc. in Mi♭
Cl. in Si♭
Cl. bas. in Si♭
Fag.
C. Fag.
Cor. in Fa
160
Vl. I
Vl. II div. a 3
Vle. div. a 3
Vc.
Cb.

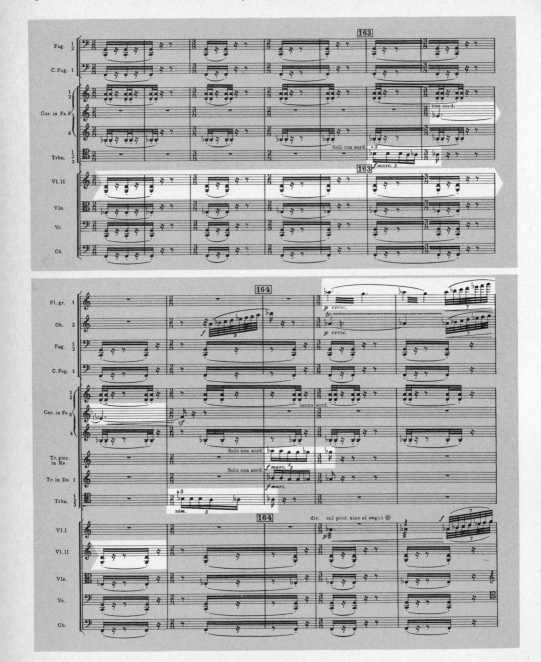

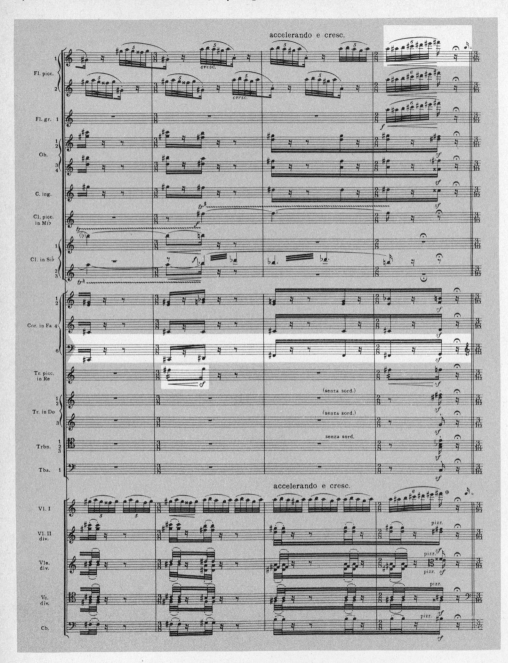

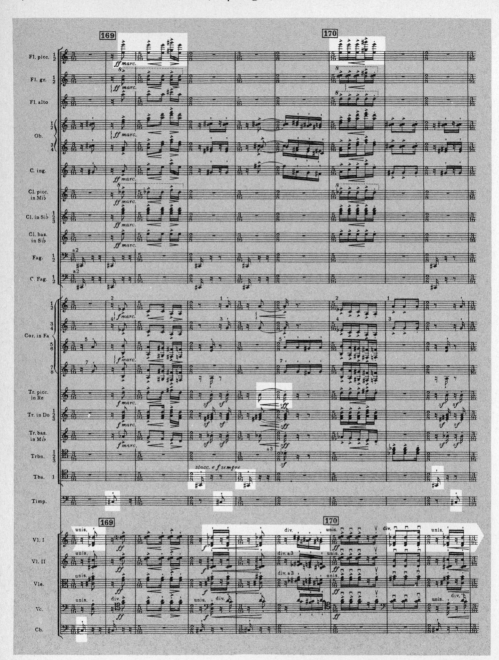

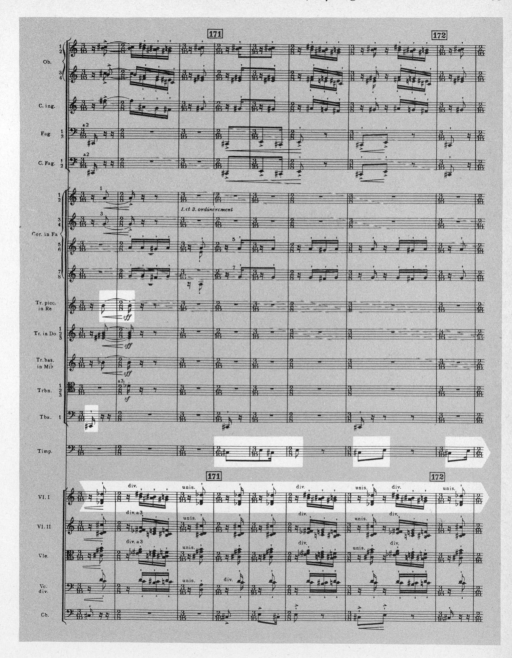

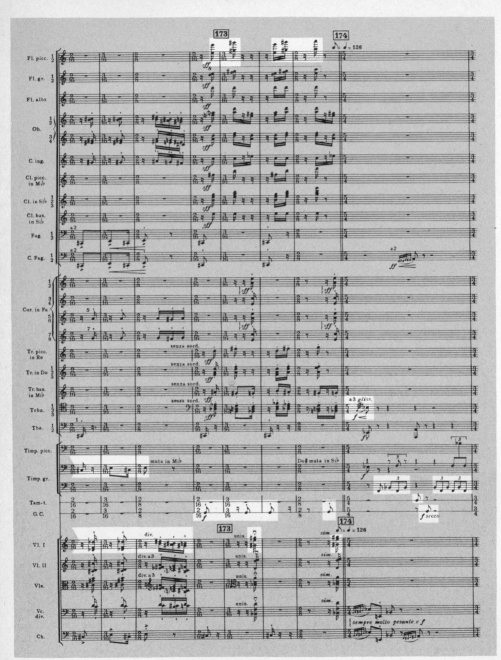

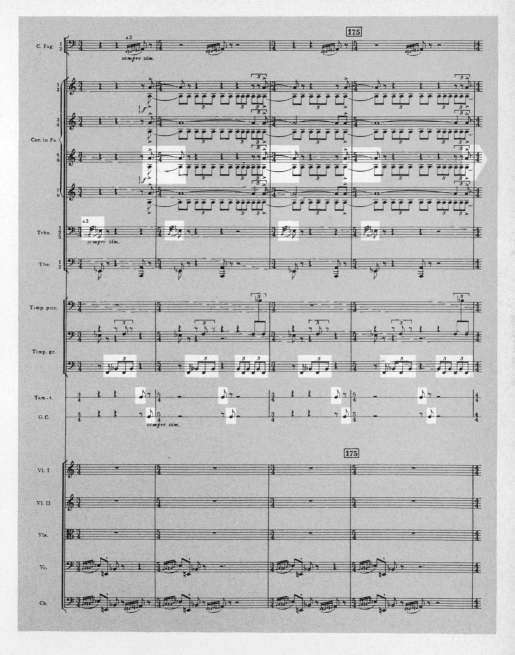

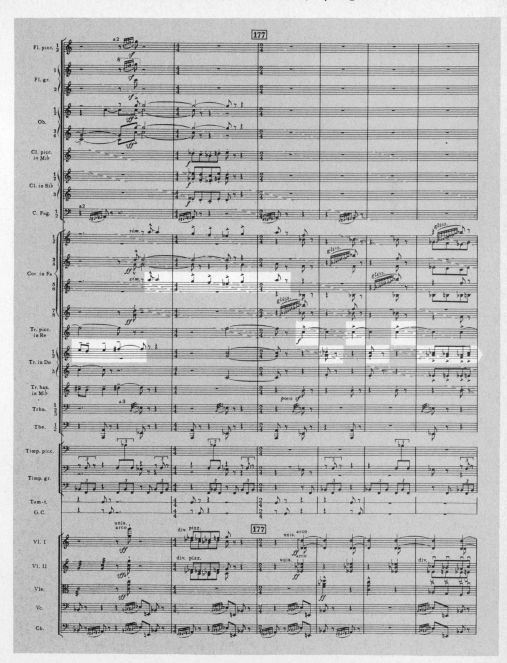

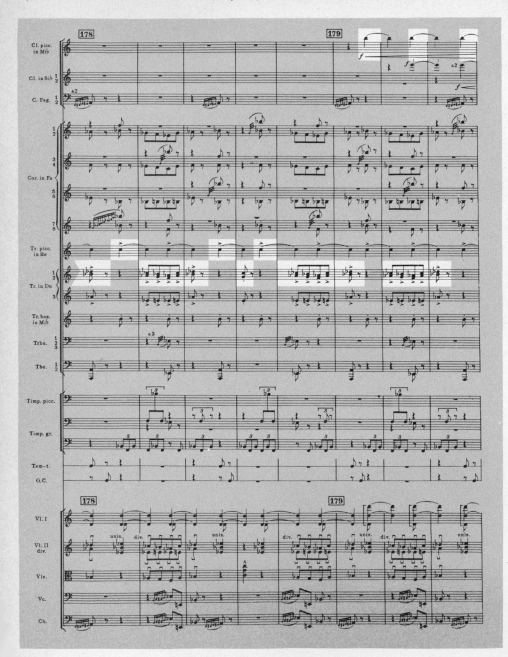

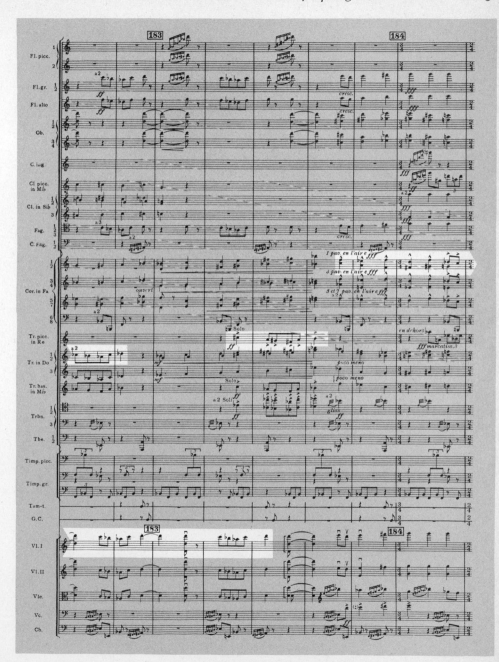

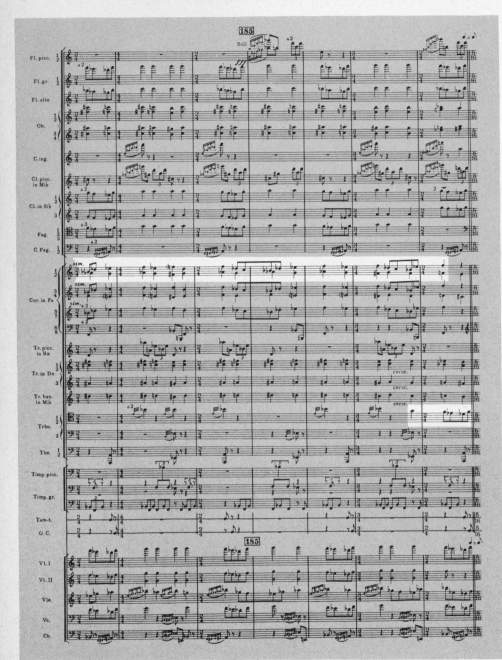

188
189
Fl. gr.
Fl. alto
Ob.
C. ing.
Cl. picc. in Mib
Cl. in Sib
Fag.
C. Fag.
a 2
fff
f marc.
Cor. in Fa
poco sf
Tr. picc. in Re
Tr. in Do
Tr. bas. in Mib
Trbn.
Tbe.
Timp.
mf
G. C.
Vl. I
Vl. II
Vle.
Vc.
Cb.
div.
div. a 3
unis.

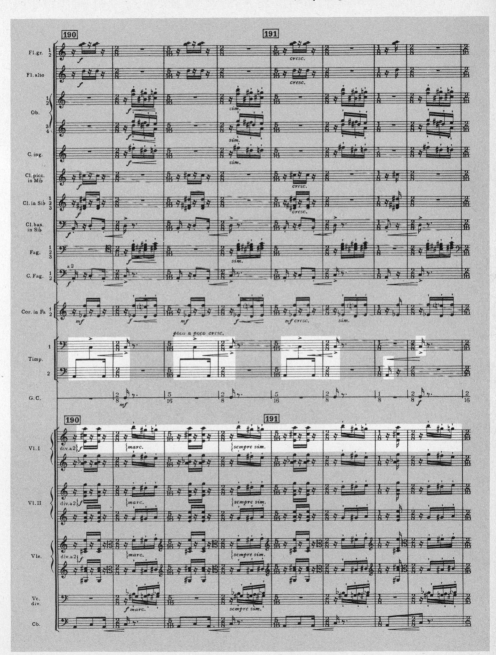

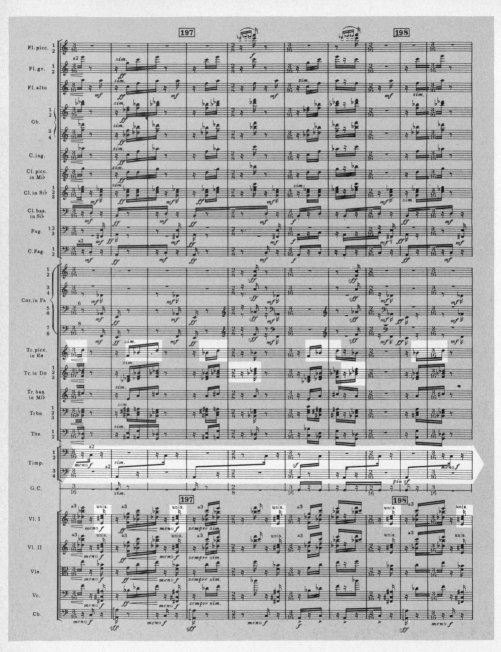

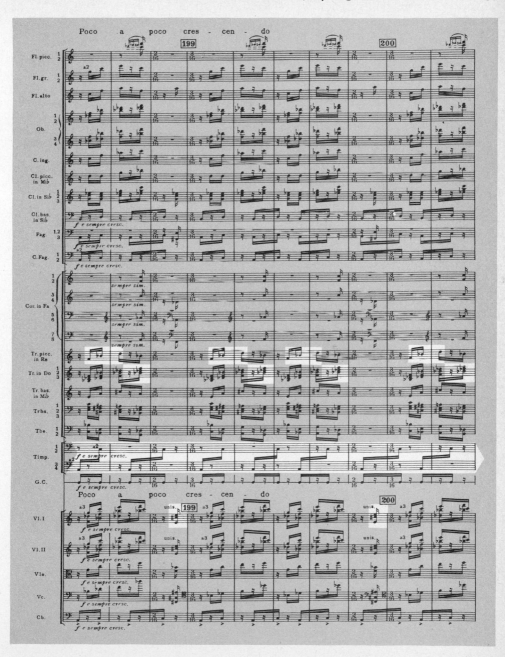

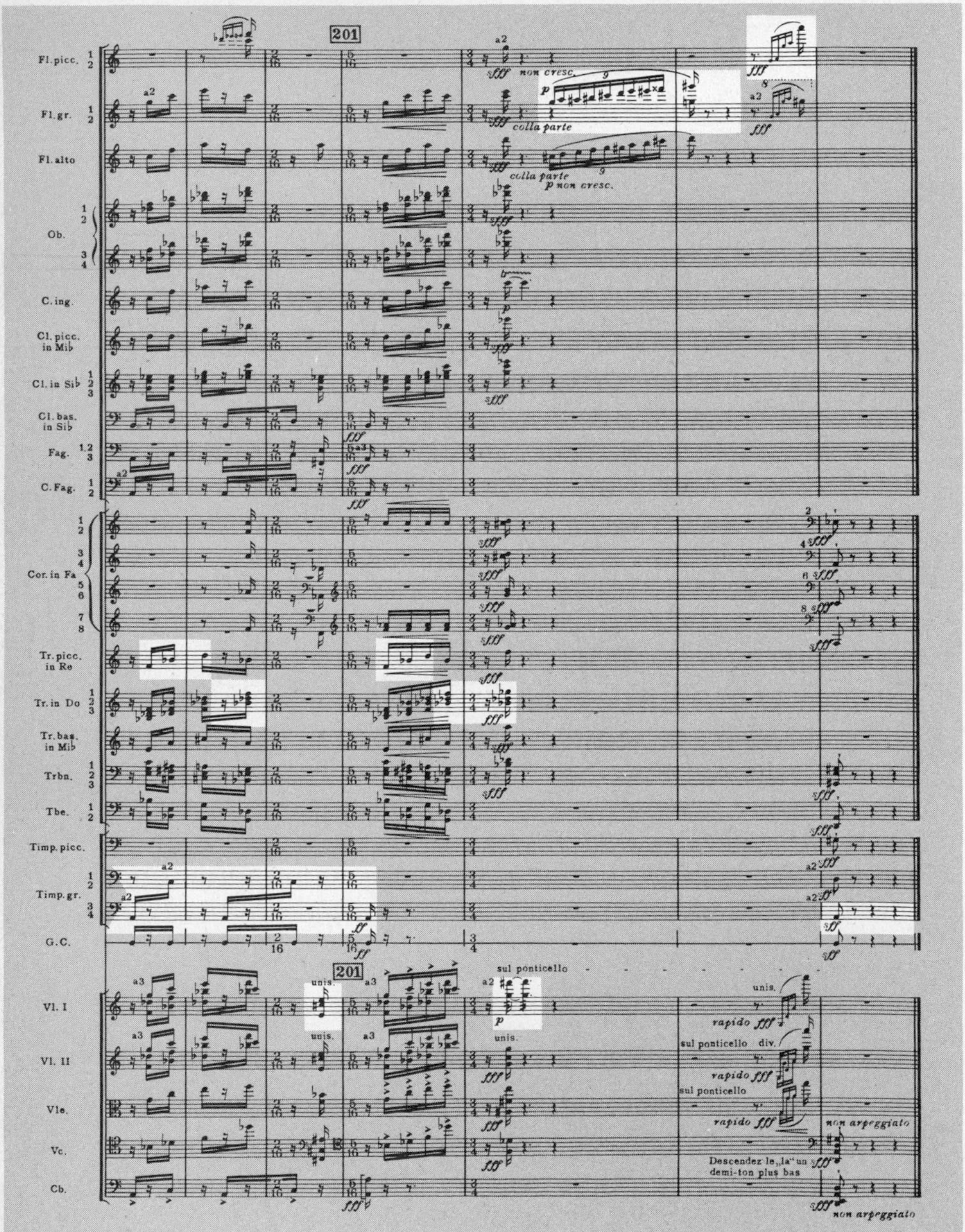
201
Fl. picc. 1 2
Fl. gr. 1 2
Fl. alto
Ob. 1 2 3 4
C. ing.
Cl. picc. in Mi♭
Cl. in Si♭ 1 2 3
Cl. bas. in Si♭
Fag. 1.2 3
C. Fag. 1 2
Cor. in Fa 1 2 3 4 5 6 7 8
Tr. picc. in Re
Tr. in Do 1 2 3
Tr. bas. in Mi♭
Trbn. 1 2 3
Tbe. 1 2
Timp. picc.
Timp. gr. 1 2 3 4
G. C.
Vl. I
Vl. II
Vle.
Vc.
Cb.
a2
a3
non cresc.
colla parte
p non cresc.
sul ponticello
unis.
div.
rapido
non arpeggiato
Descendez le „la" un demi-ton plus bas

27. STRAVINSKY, First movement from *Symphony of Psalms* (1930)

© 1931 by Russicher Musikverlag; Renewed 1958
Copyright and Renewal assigned to Boosey & Hawkes Inc.
Revised Edition © 1948 by Boosey and Hawkes Inc.
Reprinted by permission

Translation

Hear my prayer, O Lord, and give ear unto my cry;
hold not Thy peace at my tears; for I am a stranger
with Thee, and sojourner, as all my fathers were. O
spare me, that I may recover strength: before I go
hence, and be no more.

PSALM 39 (KING JAMES VERSION),
VERSES 12-13

28. ANTON WEBERN (1883-1945),
Pieces for Orchestra, Opus 10, Nos. 3 and 4 (1913)

III.

"5 Stücke für Orchester op. 10, Nr. 3 und 4", Copyright 1923 by Universal Edition A.G., Wien. Copyright Renewed 1951. Used by permission.

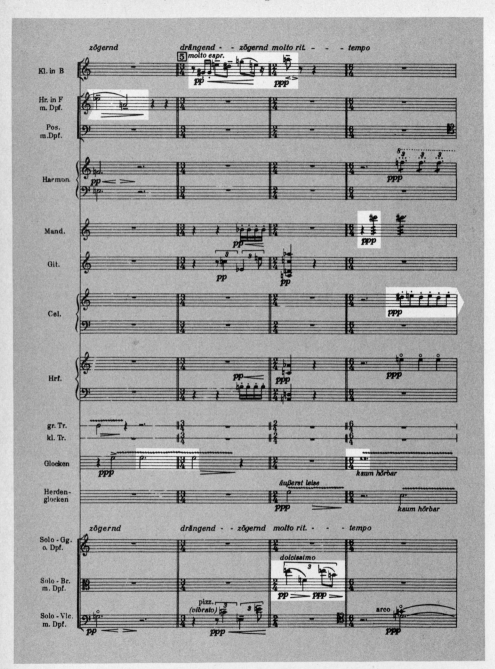

IV.

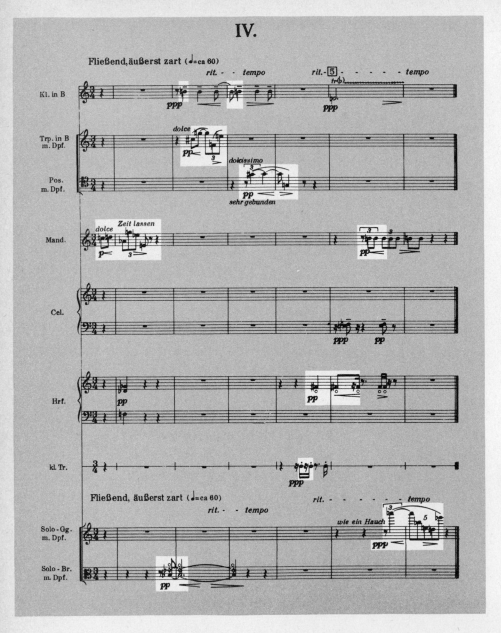

29. EDGARD VARÈSE (1883-1965), *Ionisation* (1931)

© Copyright 1934 by Edgard Varèse

© Copyright assigned 1966 to Colfranc Music Publishing Corporation, New York

© Copyright 1967 by Colfranc Music Publishing Corporation, New York

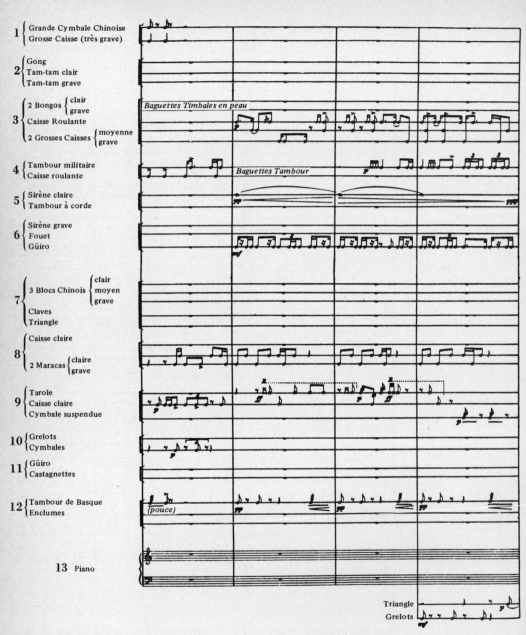

Fouet

30. ALBAN BERG (1885-1935),
Act III, Scenes 4 and 5, from *Wozzeck* (1918-1921)

Alban Berg "Wozzeck", Klavierauszug 3. Akt, Szenen 4 und 5. Copyright 1930 by Universal Edition A.G., Wien. Copyright Renewed 1958. Used by permission.

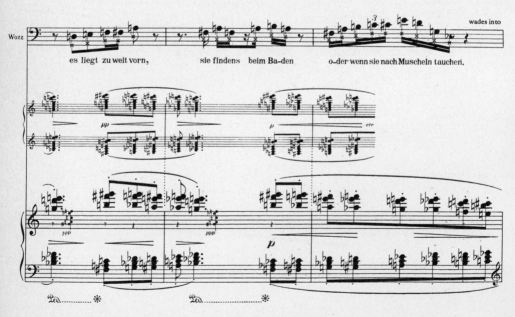

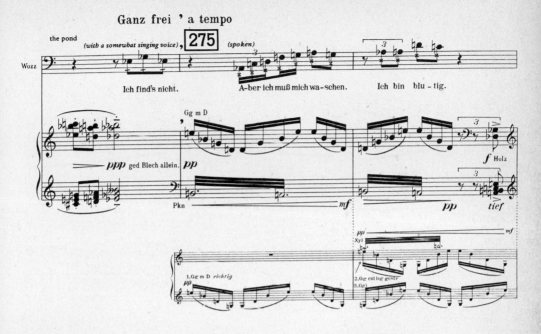

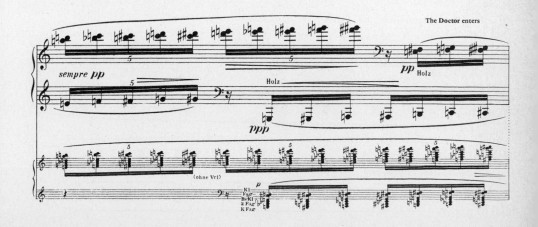

The **Captain** follows the Doctor (speaks)

The **Doctor** (stands still): *p* Hören Sie? Dort!

290 Hauptmann: *p* Jesus! Das war ein Ton. (also stands still)

Doktor (pointing to the lake): Ja, dort!   **Hauptmann:** Es ist das Wasser

im Teich. Das Wasser ruft. Es ist schon lange niemand ertrunken.

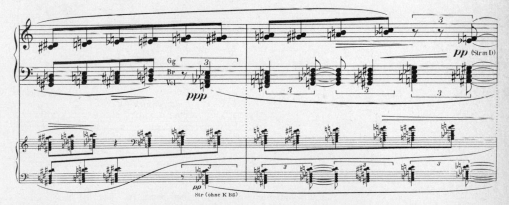

Hauptmann: Kommen Sie, Doktor! Es ist

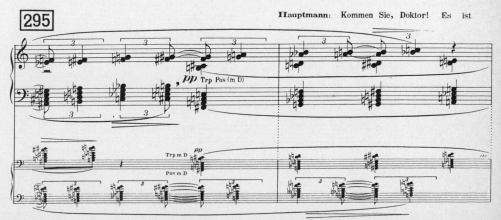

5th (last) Scene   In front of Marie's house (bright morning, sunshine)

Flowing 8ths, but with much rubato

♪ = the previous triplet

(♩. = 72 beginning)

Mariens Knabe   riding a hobby horse

End of the opera

Translation

SCENE FOUR

WOZZECK
Das Messer? Wo ist das Messer?
Ich hab's dagelassen. Näher, noch näher.

Mir graut's da regt sich was.
Still! Alles still und tot.
Mörder! Mörder!!
Ha! Da ruft's. Nein, ich selbst.
Marie! Marie! Was hast Du für eine rote
  Schnur um den Hals?
Hast Dir das rote Halsband verdient, wie die
  Ohrringlein, mit Deiner Sünde!
Was hängen Dir die schwarzen Haare so wild?!
Mörder! Mörder!!
Sie werden nach mir suchen. Das Messer verrät
  mich!
Da, da ist's! So! Da hinunter!
Es taucht ins dunkle Wasser wie ein Stein.
Aber der Mond verrät mich, der Mond ist blutig.
Will denn die ganze Welt es ausplaudern?!
Das Messer, es liegt zu weit vorn, sie finden's
  beim Baden oder wenn sie nach Muscheln
  tauchen.
Ich find's nicht. Aber ich muss mich waschen.

Ich bin blutig. Da ein Fleck und noch einer.
Weh! Weh!
Ich wasche mich mit Blut, das Wasser ist
  Blut . . . Blut . . .

WOZZECK
The knife? Where is the knife?
I left it somewhere, somewhere, here,
  somewhere.
Oh, horror, something moved there.
Still! All is still and dead.
Murder! Murder!!
Ah! Someone's calling. No, it was me.
Marie! Marie! What is that, so like a crimson
  cord around your neck?
Did you earn that crimson necklace, as you did
  those earrings, with your sinning?
Why does your black hair hang so wild?!
Murder! Murder!!
They will soon be looking for me. The knife
  will betray me!
There, there it is! There! Down to the bottom!
It sinks through the dark water like a stone.
But the moon betrays me, the moon is bloody.
Then will the whole world be blabbing it?!
The knife, it is too near the shore, they'll find
  it when they're swimming or gathering
  mussels.
I don't see it any longer. But I ought to wash
  myself.
I'm bloody. There's a spot, and here another.
Woe! Woe!
I'm washing myself with blood, the water is
  blood . . . blood . . .

DER HAUPTMANN Halt!	**THE CAPTAIN** Stop!
DER DOKTOR Hören Sie? Dort!	**THE DOCTOR** Do you hear? There!
DER HAUPTMANN Jesus! Das war ein Ton.	**THE CAPTAIN** Jesus! That was a sound.
DER DOKTOR Ja, dort!	**THE DOCTOR** Yes, there!
DER HAUPTMANN Es ist das Wasser im Teich. Das Wasser ruft. Es ist schon lange Niemand ertrunken. Kommen Sie, Doktor! Es ist nicht gut zu hören.	**THE CAPTAIN** It is the water in the pool. The water calls. It's a long time since anyone was drowned. Come, doctor! This is not a good thing to hear.
DER DOKTOR Das stöhnt als stürbe ein Mensch. Da ertrinkt Jemand!	**THE DOCTOR** It groans like a man dying. Someone's drowning there!
DER HAUPTMANN Unheimlich! Der Mond rot, und die Nebel grau. Hören Sie? Jetzt wieder das Ächzen.	**THE CAPTAIN** Uncanny! The moon is red, and the mist, grey. Do you hear? There's the groaning again.
DER DOKTOR Stiller, jetzt ganz still.	**THE DOCTOR** It's getting softer, and now all still.
DER HAUPTMANN Kommen Sie! Kommen Sie schnell!	**THE CAPTAIN** Come on! Come away quickly!

SCENE FIVE

KINDER
Ringel, Ringel, Rosenkranz, Ringelreih'n!
Ringel, Ringel, Rosenkranz, Rin—

EINS VON IHNEN
Du, Käthie! Die Marie . . .

ZWEITES KIND
Was is?

ERSTES KIND
Weisst' es nit? Sie sind schon Alle 'naus.

DRITTES KIND
Du! Dein Mutter ist tot!

MARIENS KNABE
Hopp, hopp! Hopp, hopp! Hopp, hopp!

ZWEITES KIND
Wo ist sie denn?

ERSTES KIND
Drauss' liegt sie, am Weg, neben dem Teich.

DRITTES KIND
Kommt anschaun!

MARIENS KNABE
Hopp, hopp! Hopp, hopp! Hopp, hopp!

CHILDREN
Ring a ring of roses, All fall down!
Ring a ring of roses, All—

ONE OF THE CHILDREN
Hey, Katie! Marie . . .

SECOND CHILD
What is it?

FIRST CHILD
Don't you know? They've all gone out there.

THIRD CHILD
Hey, you! Your mother is dead!

MARIE'S CHILD
Hop, hop! Hop, hop! Hop, hop!

SECOND CHILD
Where is she, then?

FIRST CHILD
She's out there, on the path, by the pool.

THIRD CHILD
Let's go and look!

MARIE'S CHILD
Hop, hop! Hop, hop! Hop, hop!

31. AARON COPLAND (b. 1900),
Opening scene from *Billy the Kid* (1938)

Copyright 1941 by Aaron Copland; Renewed 1968. Reprinted by permission of Aaron Copland, and Boosey & Hawkes, Inc., Sole Licensees.

Picc.
Fl. 1 2
Ob. 1 2
Clar. 1 2
Bsn 1 2
Hr.
Trpt 1 2 3
Trb. 1 2 3
Tb.
Timp.
B.Drum.
Harp.
Piano
Vl. 1 2
Vla.
Vlc.
Cb.
solo
p cantabile
soli
p poco marc.
con sordino
p poco marc.
pp
ppp
pp
1
unis
p poco marc.
unis.
p poco marc.
p poco marcato

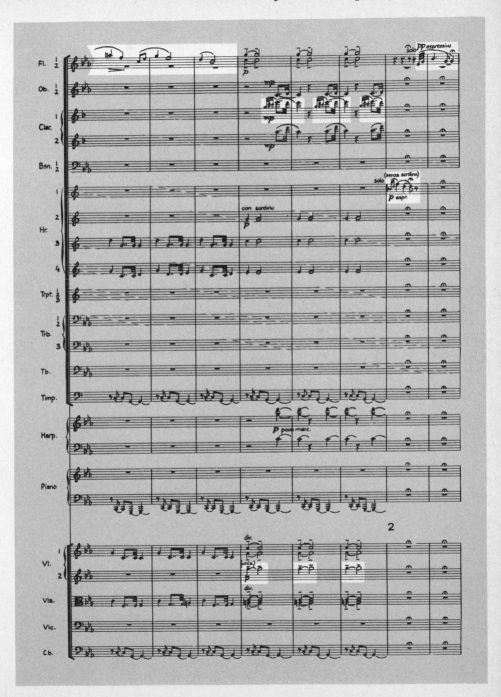

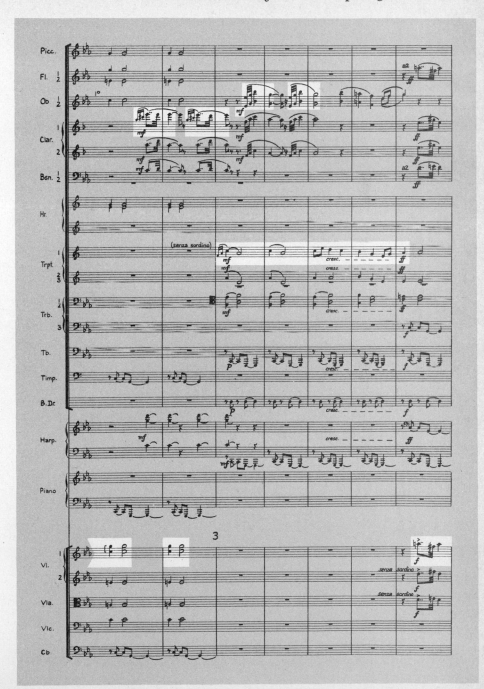

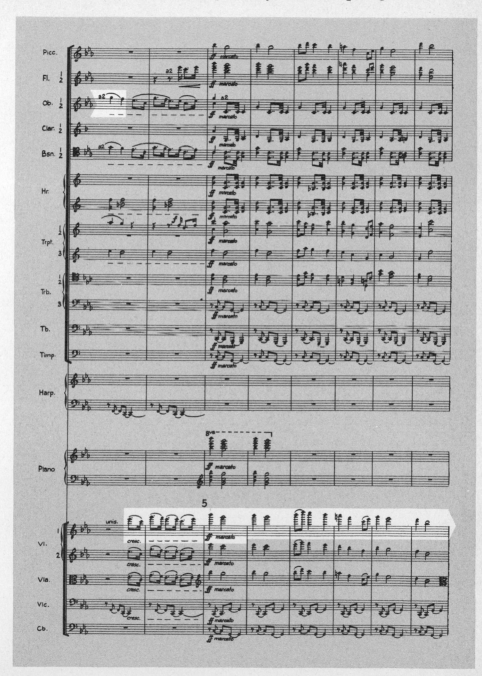

32. RUTH CRAWFORD (1901-1953),
Third movement from *String Quartet 1931*

The dotted ties ·‑ ‑ ‑ ‑ ‑ indicate that the first tone of each new bow is not to be attacked;
the bowing should be as little audible as possible throughout.
The crescendi and decrescendi should be equally gradual.

Copyright 1941, Merion Music, Inc. Used by permission.

* The half notes in measures 85-88 should be faster than the quarter notes in measure 77.

33. ELLIOTT CARTER (b. 1908), Etudes 4, 5, and 8 from *Eight Etudes and a Fantasy for Woodwind Quartet* (1950)

IV

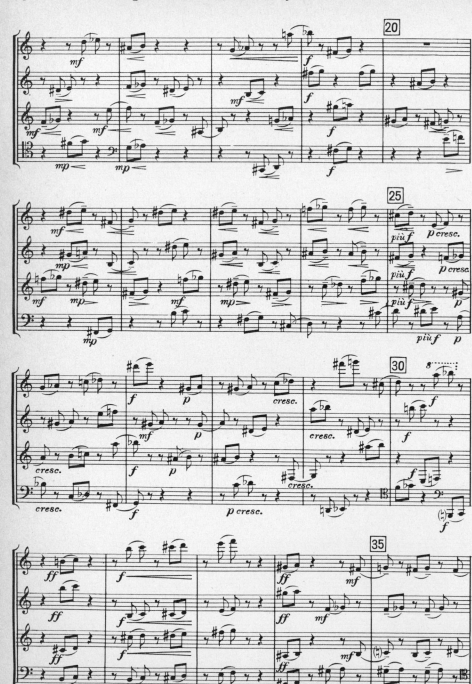

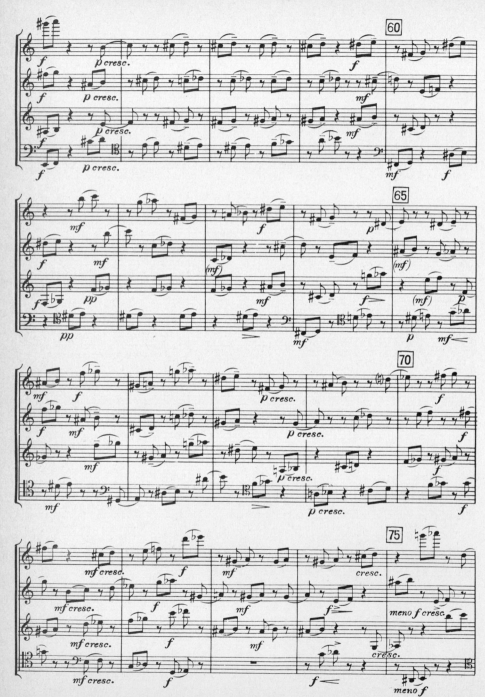

V

VIII

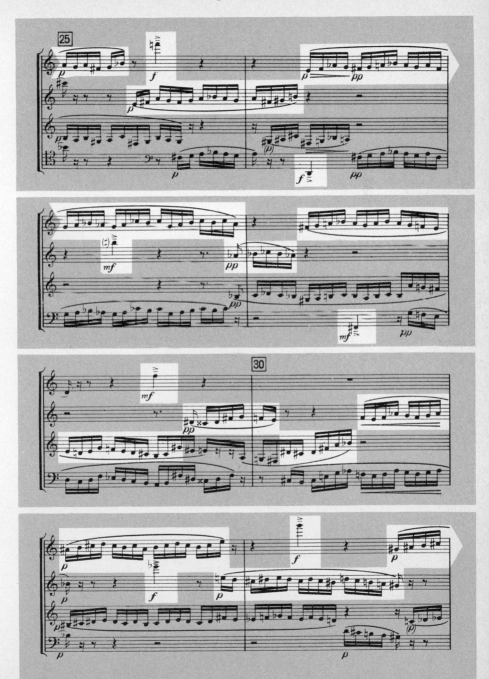

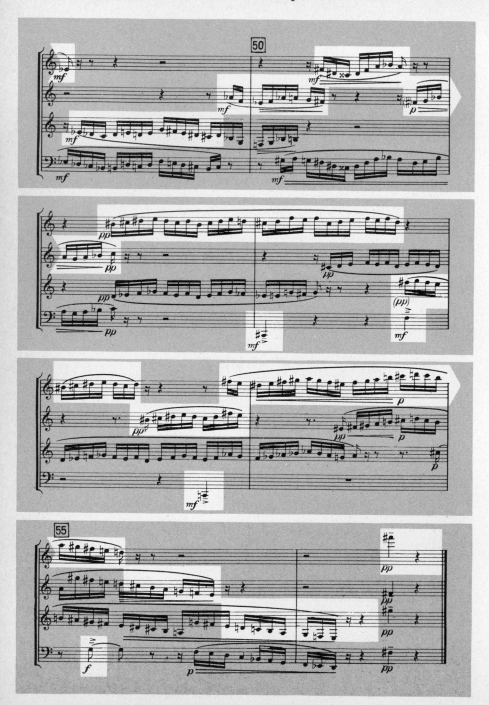

34. PIERRE BOULEZ (b. 1925), Excerpts from *Le Marteau sans maître*

No. 1: *Before "L'Artisanat furieux"*

Pierre Boulez "Le marteau sans maître, Nr. 1, 3 und 7", Copyright 1954 by Universal Edition (London) Ltd., London. Final Version: Copyright 1957 by Universal Edition (London) Ltd., London. Poèmes de René Char: Copyright by José Corti Editeur, Paris. Used by permission.

No. 3: *"L'Artisanat furieux"*

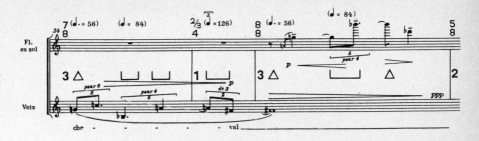

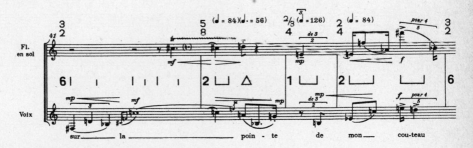

Translation

La roulotte fouge au bord du clou
Et cadavre dans le panier
Et chevaux de labours dans le fer à cheval
Je rêve la tête sur la pointe de mon couteau le
  Pérou

The red caravan at the edge of the prison
And a corpse in the basket
And a workhorse in the horseshoe
I dream, head on the point of my knife, Peru

No. 7: After "L'Artisanat furieux"

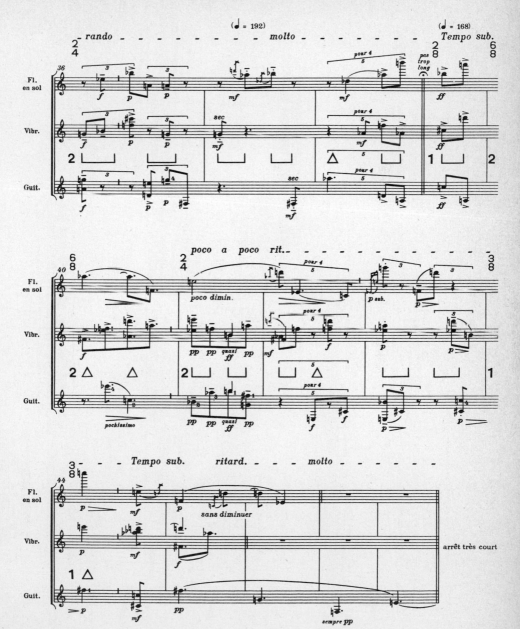

35. GEORGE CRUMB (b. 1929),
El niño busca su voz from Ancient Voices of Children (1970)

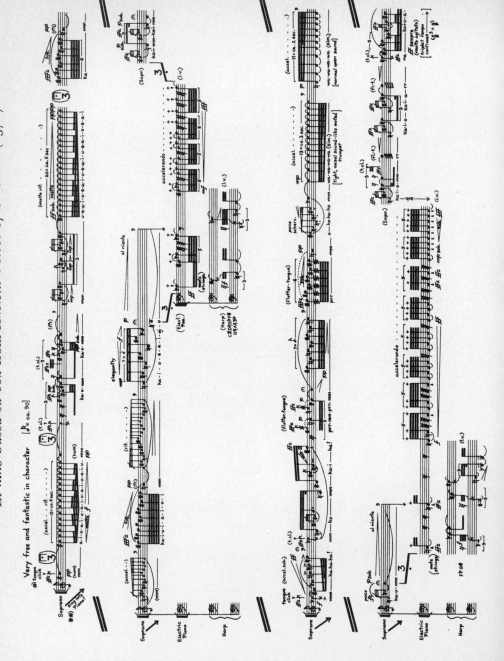

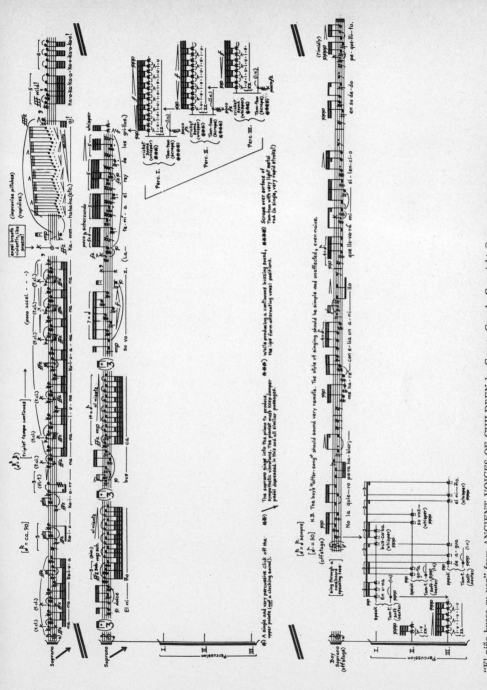

"El niño busca su voz" from ANCIENT VOICES OF CHILDREN by George Crumb. Copyright © 1970 by C. F. Peters Corporation, 373 Park Avenue South, New York 10016. Reprinted with permission of the publishers who published the score of the complete work under Peters Edition No. 66303.

Translation

El niño busca su voz.	The little boy was looking for his voice.
(La tenía el rey de los grillos.)	(The king of the crickets had it.)
En una gota de agua	In a drop of water
buscaba su voz el niño.	the little boy was looking for his voice.
No la quiero para hablar;	I do not want it for speaking with;
me haré con ella un anillo	I will make a ring of it
que llevará mi silencio	so that he may wear my silence
en su dedo pequeñito.	on his little finger.

TEXT BY FEDERICO GARCÍA LORCA;
TRANSLATION BY W. S. MERWIN

36. MARIO DAVIDOVSKY (b. 1934),
Synchronisms No. 1 for Flute and Electronic Sounds (1963)

Copyright © 1966 by Josef Marx, McGinnis & Marx Music Publishers, 201 West 86th Street, New York, New York 10024; used by permission.

Start this part, right after electronic cue ♯ 3, is finished.

⊕ = Air + Percussion   + = Percussion only.

Appendix A

Reading an Orchestral Score

CLEFS

The music for some instruments is written in clefs other than the familiar treble and bass. In the following example, middle C is shown in the four clefs used in orchestral scores:

Treble   Alto   Tenor   Bass
clef   clef   clef   clef

The *alto clef* is primarily used in viola parts. The *tenor clef* is employed for cello, bassoon, and trombone parts when these instruments play in a high register.

TRANSPOSING INSTRUMENTS

The music for some instruments is customarily written at a pitch different from their actual sound. The following list, with examples, shows the main transposing instruments and the degree of transposition. (In some modern works—such as the Schoenberg example included in this anthology —all instruments are written at their sounding pitch.)

Instrument	Transposition	Written Note	Actual Sound

Piccolo
  Celesta
	sound an octave
	  higher than written		

Trumpet in F	sound a fourth higher than written.		
Trumpet in E	sound a major third higher than written		

Instrument	Transposition	Written Note	Actual Sound
Clarinet in Eb Trumpet in Eb	sound a minor third higher than written		
Trumpet in D Clarinet in D	sound a major second higher than written		
Clarinet in Bb Trumpet in Bb Cornet in Bb Horn in Bb alto	sound a major second lower than written		
Clarinet in A Trumpet in A Cornet in A	sound a minor third lower than written		
Horn in G Alto flute	sound a fourth lower than written		
English horn Horn in F	sound a fifth lower than written		
Horn in E	sound a minor sixth lower than written		
Horn in Eb	sound a major sixth lower than written		
Horn in D	sound a minor seventh lower than written		
Contrabassoon Horn in C Double bass	sound an octave lower than written		
Bass clarinet in Bb (written in treble clef)	sound a major ninth lower than written		
(written in bass clef)	sound a major second lower than written		
Bass clarinet in A (written in treble clef)	sound a minor tenth lower than written		
(written in bass clef)	sound a minor third lower than written		

Appendix B

Instrumental Names and Abbreviations

The following tables set forth the English, Italian, German, and French names used for the various musical instruments in these scores, and their respective abbreviations. A table of the foreign-language names for scale degrees and modes is also provided.

WOODWINDS

English	Italian	German	French
Piccolo (Picc.)	Flauto piccolo (Fl. Picc.)	Kleine Flöte (Kl. Fl.)	Petite flûte
Flute (Fl.)	Flauto (Fl.); Flauto grande (Fl. gr.)	Grosse Flöte (Fl. gr.)	Flûte (Fl.)
Alto flute	Flauto contralto (fl.c-alto)	Altflöte	Flûte en sol
Oboe (Ob.)	Oboe (Ob.)	Hoboe (Hb.); Oboe (Ob.)	Hautbois (Hb.)
English horn (E. H.)	Corno inglese (C. or Cor. ingl., C.i.)	Englisches Horn (E. H.)	Cor anglais (C. A.)
Sopranino clarinet	Clarinetto piccolo (clar. picc.)		
Clarinet (C., Cl., Clt., Clar.)	Clarinetto (Cl. Clar.)	Klarinette (Kl.)	Clarinette (Cl.)
Bass clarinet (B. Cl.)	Clarinetto basso (Cl. b., Cl. basso, Clar. basso)	Bass Klarinette (Bkl.)	Clarinette basse (Cl. bs.)
Bassoon (Bsn., Bssn.)	Fagotto (Fag., Fg.)	Fagott (Fag., Fg.)	Basson (Bssn.)
Contrabassoon (C. Bsn.)	Contrafagotto (Cfg., C. Fag., Cont. F.)	Kontrafagott (Kfg.)	Contrebasson (C. bssn.)

BRASS

English	Italian	German	French
French horn (Hr., Hn.)	Corno (Cor., C.)	Horn (Hr.) [*pl.* Hörner (Hrn.)]	Cor; Cor à pistons
Trumpet (Tpt., Trpt., Trp., Tr.)	Tromba (Tr.)	Trompete (Tr., Trp.)	Trompette (Tr.)
Trumpet in D	Tromba piccola (Tr. picc.)		
Cornet	Cornetta	Kornett	Cornet à pistons (C. à p., Pist.)
Trombone (Tr., Tbe., Trb., Trm., Trbe.)	Trombone [*pl.* Tromboni (Tbni., Trni.)]	Posaune.(Ps., Pos.)	Trombone (Tr.)
Tuba (Tb.)	Tuba (Tb, Tba₁)	Tuba (Tb.) [*also* Basstuba (Btb.)]	Tuba (Tb.)

PERCUSSION

English	Italian	German	French
Percussion (Perc.)	Percussione	Schlagzeug (Schlag.)	Batterie (Batt.)
Kettledrums (K. D.)	Timpani (Timp., Tp.)	Pauken (Pk.)	Timbales (Timb.)
Snare drum (S. D.)	Tamburo piccolo (Tamb. picc.) Tamburo militare (Tamb. milit.)	Kleine Trommel (Kl. Tr.)	Caisse claire (C. cl.), Caisse roulante Tambour militaire (Tamb. milit.)
Bass drum (B. drum)	Gran cassa (Gr. Cassa, Gr. C., G. C.)	Grosse Trommel (Gr. Tr.)	Grosse caisse (Gr. c.)
Cymbals (Cym., Cymb.)	Piatti (P., Ptti., Piat.)	Becken (Beck.)	Cymbales (Cym.)
Tam-Tam (Tam-T.)			
Tambourine (Tamb.)	Tamburino (Tamb.)	Schellentrommel, Tamburin	Tambour de Basque (T. de B., Tamb. de Basque)

Triangle (Trgl., Tri.)	Triangolo (Trgl.)	Triangel	Triangle (Triang.)
Glockenspiel (Glocken.)	Campanelli (Cmp.)	Glockenspiel	Carillon
Bells (Chimes)	Campane (Cmp.)	Glocken	Cloches
Antique Cymbals	Crotali Piatti antichi	Antiken Zimbeln	Cymbales antiques
Sleigh Bells	Sonagli (Son.)	Schellen	Grelots
Xylophone (Xyl.)	Xilofono	Xylophon	Xylophone
Cowbells		Herdenglocken	
Crash cymbal			Grande cymbale chinoise
Siren			Sirène
Lion's roar			Tambour à corde
Slapstick			Fouet
Wood blocks			Blocs chinois

STRINGS

English	Italian	German	French
Violin (V., Vl., Vln, Vi.)	Violino (V., Vl., Vln.)	Violine (V., Vl., Vln.) Geige (Gg.)	Violon (V., Vl., Vln.)
Viola (Va., Vl., *pl.* Vas.)	Viola (Va., Vla.) *pl.* Viole (Vle.)	Bratsche (Br.)	Alto (A.)
Violoncello, Cello (Vcl., Vc.)	Violoncello (Vc., Vlc., Vcllo.)	Violoncell (Vc., Vlc.)	Violoncelle (Vc.)
Double bass (D. Bs.)	Contrabasso (Cb., C. B.) *pl.* Contrabassi or Bassi (C. Bassi, Bi.)	Kontrabass (Kb.)	Contrebasse (C. B.)

OTHER INSTRUMENTS

English	Italian	German	French
Harp (Hp., Hrp.)	Arpa (A., Arp.)	Harfe (Hrf.)	Harpe (Hp.)
Piano	Pianoforte (P.-f., Pft.)	Klavier	Piano
Celesta (Cel.)			
Harpsichord	Cembalo	Cembalo	Clavecin
Harmonium (Harmon.)			
Organ (Org.)	Organo	Orgel	Orgue
Guitar		Gitarre (Git.)	
Mandoline (Mand.)			

Names of Scale Degrees and Modes

SCALE DEGREES

English	Italian	German	French
C	do	C	ut
C-sharp	do diesis	Cis	ut dièse
D-flat	re bemolle	Des	ré bémol
D	re	D	ré
D-sharp	re diesis	Dis	ré dièse
E-flat	mi bemolle	Es	mi bémol
E	mi	E	mi
E-sharp	mi diesis	Eis	mi dièse
F-flat	fa bemolle	Fes	fa bémol
F	fa	F	fa
F-sharp	fa diesis	Fis	fa dièse
G-flat	sol bemolle	Ges	sol bémol
G	sol	G	sol
G-sharp	sol diesis	Gis	sol dièse
A-flat	la bemolle	As	la bémol
A	la	A	la
A-sharp	la diesis	Ais	la dièse
B-flat	si bemolle	B	si bémol
B	si	H	si
B-sharp	si diesis	His	si dièse
C-flat	do bemolle	Ces	ut bémol

MODES

major	maggiore	dur	majeur
minor	minore	moll	mineur

Appendix C

Glossary of Musical Terms Used in the Scores

The following glossary is not intended to be a complete dictionary of musical terms, nor is knowledge of all these terms necessary to follow the scores in this book. However, as the listener gains experience in following scores, he will find it useful and interesting to understand the composer's directions with regard to tempo, dynamics, and methods of performance.

In most cases, compound terms have been broken down in the glossary and defined separately, as they often recur in varying combinations. A few common foreign-language particles are included in addition to the musical terms. Note that names and abbreviations for instruments and for scale degrees will be found in Appendix B.

a. The phrases *a 2, a 3* (etc.) indicate that the part is to be played in unison by 2, 3 (etc.) players; when a simple number (1., 2., etc.) is placed over a part, it indicates that only the first (second, etc.) player in that group should play.

aber. But.

accelerando. Growing faster.

accentué. Accented.

accompagnato (accomp.). In a continuo part, this indicates that the chord-playing instrument resumes (cf. *tasto solo*).

accordez. Tune the instrument as specified.

adagio. Slow, leisurely.

ad libitum (ad lib.). An indication giving the performer liberty to: (1) vary from strict tempo; (2) include or omit the part of some voice or in-strument; (3) include a cadenza of his own invention.

affettuoso. With emotion.

affrettando (affrett.). Hastening a little.

agitato. Agitated, excited.

agitazione. Agitation.

allargando (allarg.). Growing broader.

alle, alles. All, every, each.

allegretto. A moderately fast tempo (between allegro and andante).

allegro. A rapid tempo (between allegretto and presto).

allein. Alone, solo.

allmählich. Gradually (*allmählich gleichmässig fliessend werden,* gradually becoming even-flowing again).

al niente. Reduce to nothing.

alto, altus (A.). The deeper of the two main divisions of women's (or boys') voices.

am Steg. On the bridge (of a string instrument).

ancora. Again.

andante. A moderately slow tempo (between adagio and allegretto).

andantino. A moderately slow tempo.

an dem Griffbrett (a.d.G.). Played on the fingerboard.

anima. Spirit, animation.

animando. With increasing animation.

animato, animé. Animated.

a piacere. The execution of the passage is left to the performer's discretion.

à plat. Laid flat.

appassionato. Impassioned.

arco. Played with the bow.

arditamente. Boldly.

armonioso. Harmoniously.

arpeggiando, arpeggiato (arpeg.). Played in harp style, i.e. the notes of the chord played in quick succession rather than simultaneously.

arrêt. Stop.

assai. Very.

a tempo. At the (basic) tempo.

attacca. Begin what follows without pausing.

attaque sèche. Sharp attack.

auf dem. On the (as in *auf dem G,* on the G string).

Ausdruck. Expression.

ausdrucksvoll. With expression.

bachetti. Drumsticks (*bachetti di tamburo militare,* snare-drum sticks; *bachetti di spugna,* sponge-headed drumsticks).

baguettes. Drumsticks (*baguettes de bois, baguettes timbales de bois,* wooden drumsticks or kettledrum sticks; *baguettes d'éponge,* sponge-headed drumsticks; *baguettes midures,* semi-hard drumsticks; *baguettes dures,* hard drumsticks; *baguettes timbales en feutre,* felt-headed kettledrum sticks).

bass, basso, bassus (B.). The lowest male voice.

battuto coll' arco. Struck with the bow.

beaucoup. Many, much.

bedeutung bewegter. With significantly more movement.

beide Hände. With both hands.

belebend. With increasing animation.

belebt. Animated.

ben. Very.

ben accordato. Well tuned.

bestimmt. Energetic.

bewegt. Agitated.

bewegter. More agitated.

bien. Very.

bis zum Schluss dieser Szene. To the end of this scene.

Blech. Brass instruments.

Bogen (Bog.). Played with the bow.

bouché. Muted.

bravura. Boldness.

breit. Broadly.

breiter. More broadly.

brillante. Brilliant.

brio. Spirit, vivacity.

cadenza. An extended passage for solo instrument in free, improvisatory style.

calando. Diminishing in volume and speed.

calma, calmo. Calm, calmly.

cantabile (cant.). In a singing style.

cantando. In a singing manner.

canto. Voice (as in *col canto,* a direction for the accompaniment to follow the solo part in tempo and expression).

cantus. An older designation for the highest part in a vocal work.

capella. Choir, chorus.

cédez. Go a little slower.

changez. Change (usually an instruction to re-tune a string or an instrument).

circa (ca.). About, approximately.

clair. High.

col, colla, coll'. With the.

come prima, come sopra. As at first; as previously.

con. With.

corda. String; for example, *seconda (2a) corda* is the second string (the A string on the violin).

coro. Chorus.

coulisse. Wings (of a theater).

court. Short, staccato.

crescendo (cresc.). An increase in volume.

cuivré. Played with a harsh, blaring tone.

cum quatuor vocibus. With four voices.

cupo. Dark, veiled.

da capo (D.C.). Repeat from the beginning.

dal segno. Repeat from the sign.

Dämpfer (Dpf.). Mutes.

dans. In.

dazu. In addition to that, for that purpose.

début. Beginning.

decrescendo (decresc., decr.). A decreasing of volume.

descendez le "la" un demi-ton plus bas. Lower the A-string a semitone.

détaché. With a broad, vigorous bow stroke, each note bowed singly.

détimbrée. With snares (of a snare drum) relaxed.

deutlich. Distinctly.

dimenuendo, diminuer (dim., dimin.). A decreasing of volume.

distinto. Distinct, clear.

divisés, divisi (div.). Divided; indicates that the instrumental group should be divided into two parts to play the passage in question.

dolce. Sweetly and softly.

dolcemente. Sweetly.

dolcissimo (dolciss.). Very sweetly.

Doppelgriff. Double stop.

doppio movimento. Twice as fast.

doux. Sweetly.

drängend. Pressing on.

duplum. In older music, the part immediately above the tenor.

durée indiquée. The duration indicated.

e. And.

eilen. To hurry.

en animant. Becoming more animated.

enchainez. Continue to the next material without pause.

en dehors. With emphasis.

energico. Energetically.

ersterbend. Dying away.

erstes Tempo. At the original tempo.

espansione. Expansion, broadening.

espressione intensa. Intense expression.

espressivo (espress., espr.). Expressively.

et. And.

etwas. Somewhat, rather.

expressif. Expressively.

fehlende Akkordtöne. Missing chord tones.

fiero. Fiercely.

fine. End, close.

Flageolett (Flag.). Harmonics.

flatterzunge, flutter-tongue. A special tonguing technique for wind instruments, producing a rapid trill-like sound.

fliessend. Flowing.

forte (f). Loud.

fortissimo (ff). Very loud (*fff* indicates a still louder dynamic).

forza. Force.

frei. Freely.

freihäng. Hanging freely. An indication to the percussionist to let the cymbals vibrate feely.

frottez. Rub.

fuga. Fugue.

fuoco. Fire, spirit.

furioso. Furiously.

gajo. Gaily.

ganz. Entirely, altogether.

ganzton. Whole tone.

gedämpft (ged.). Muted.

geheimnisvoll. Mysteriously.

gesteigert. Intensified.

gestopft (chiuso). Stopping the notes of a horn; that is, the hand is placed in the bell of the horn, to produce a muffled sound.

geteilt (get.). Divided; indicates that the instrumental group should be divided into two parts to play the passage in question.

giocoso. Jocose, humorous.

giusto. Moderately.

gli altri. The others.

glissando (gliss.). Rapid scales produced by running the fingers over all the strings.

gradamente. Gradually.

grande. Large, great.

grande taille. Large size.

grave. Slow, solemn; deep, low.

grazioso. Gracefully.

grosser Auftakt. Big upbeat.

gut gehalten. Well sustained.

H. A symbol used in the music of Schoenberg, Berg, and Webern to indicate the most important voice in the texture.

Hälfte. Half.

harmonic (harm.). A flute-like sound produced on a string instrument by lightly touching the string with the finger instead of pressing it down.

Hauptzeitmass. Original tempo.

heimlich. Furtively.

hervortretend. Prominent.

hoch. High; nobly.

Holz. Woodwinds.

im gleichen Rhythmus. In the same rhythm.

immer chromatisch. Always chromatic.

immer im Tempo. Always in tempo.

in neuen Tempo. In the new tempo.

istesso tempo. Duration of beat remains unaltered despite meter change.

jeté. With a bouncing motion of the bow.

jusqu'à la fin. To the end.

kadenzieren. To cadence.

kaum hörbar. Barely audible.

klagend. Lamenting.

kurz. Short.

laissez vibrer. Let vibrate; an indication to the player of a harp, cymbal, etc., that the sound must not be damped.

langsam. Slow.

langsamer. Slower.

languente. Languishing.

langueur. Languor.

largamente. Broadly.

larghetto. Slightly faster than largo.

largo. A very slow tempo.

lebhaft. Lively.

leere Bühne. Empty stage.

legatissimo. A more forceful indication of *legato.*

legato. Performed without any perceptible interruption between notes.

légèrement. Lightly.

leggèro, leggiero (legg.). Light and graceful.

legno. The wood of the bow (*col legno tratto,* bowed with the wood; *col legno battuto,* tapped with the wood; *col legno gestrich,* played with the wood).

leise. Soft, low.

lent. Slowly.

lentamente. Slowly.

lento. A slow tempo (between andante and largo).

l.h. Abbreviation for "left hand."

lieblich. Lovely, sweetly.

loco. Indicates a return to the written pitch, following a passage played an octave higher or lower than written.

lontano. Far away, from a distance.

luftpause. Pause for breath.

lunga. Long, sustained.

lungo silenzio. A long pause.

ma. But.

maestoso. Majestic.

manual. A keyboard played with the hands (as distinct from the pedal keyboard on an organ).

marcatissimo (marcatiss.). With very marked emphasis.

marcato (marc.). Marked, with emphasis.

marcia. March.

marqué. Marked, with emphasis.

mässig. Moderate.

même. Same.

meno. Less.

mezza voce. With half the voice power.

mezzo forte (mf). Moderately loud.

mezzo piano (mp). Moderately soft.

mindistens. At least.

minore. In the minor mode.

mit. With.

M. M. Metronome; followed by an indication of the setting for the correct tempo.

moderato, modéré. At a moderate tempo.

modo ordinario (ordin.). In the usual way (usually cancelling an instruction to play using some special technique).

molto. Very, much.

morendo. Dying away.

mormorato. Murmured.

mosso. Rapid.

motetus. In medieval polyphonic music, a voice part above the tenor; generally, the first additional part to be composed.

moto. Motion.

mouvement (mouvt.). Tempo.

moyenne. Medium.

muta, mutano. Change the tuning of the instrument as specified.

N. A symbol used in the music of Schoenberg, Berg, and Webern to indicate the second most important voice in the texture.

nachgebend. Becoming slower.

nach und nach. More and more.

naturalezza. A natural, unaffected manner.

naturel. In the usual way (generally cancelling an instruction to play using some special technique).

nicht, non. Not.

noch. Still.

nuances. Shadings, expression.

oberer. Upper, leading.

octava (8va). Octave; if not otherwise qualified, means the notes marked should be played an octave higher than written.

octava bassa (8va bassa). Play an octave lower than written.

ohne. Without.

open. (1) In brass instruments, the opposite of muted; (2) in string instruments, refers to the unstopped string (i.e. sounding at its full length).

ordinario, ordinérement (ordin.). In the usual way (generally cancelling an instruction to play using some special technique).

ossia. An alternative (usually easier) version of a passage.

ôtez vite les sourdines. Remove the mutes quickly.

ouvert. Open.

parlante. Sung in a manner resembling speech.

parte. Part (*colla parte,* the accompaniment is to follow the soloist in tempo).

pas trop long. Not too long.

Paukenschlägel. Timpani stick.

pavillon en l'aire. An indication to the player of a wind instrument to raise the bell of the instrument upward.

pedal (ped., P.). (1) In piano music, indicates that the damper pedal should be depressed; an asterisk indicates the point of release (brackets below the music are also used to indicate pedalling); (2) on an organ, the pedals are a keyboard played with the feet.

percutée. Percussive.

perdendosi. Gradually dying away.

pesante. Heavily.

peu. Little, a little.

pianissimo (pp). Very soft (*ppp* indicates a still softer dynamic).

piano (p). Soft.

più. More.

pizzicato (pizz.). The string plucked with the finger.

plötzlich. Suddenly, immediately.

plus. More.

pochissimo (pochiss.). Very little, a very little.

poco. Little, a little.

poco a poco. Little by little.

ponticello (pont.). The bridge (of a string instrument).

portando la voce. With a smooth sliding of the voice from one tone to the next.

position naturel (pos. nat.). In the normal position (usually cancelling an instruction to play using some special technique).

pouce. Thumb.

pour. For.

praeludium. Prelude.

premier mouvement (1er mouvt.). At the original tempo.

prenez. Take up.

préparez le ton. Prepare the instrument to play in the key named.

presser. To press.

presto. A very quick tempo (faster than allegro).

principale (pr.). Principal, solo.

punta d'arco. Played with the top of the bow.

quasi. Almost, as if.

quasi niente. Almost nothing, i.e. as softly as possible.

quasi trill (tr.). In the manner of a trill.

quintus. An older designation for the fifth part in a vocal work.

rallentando (rall., rallent.). Growing slower.

rapide, rapido. Quick.

rapidissimo. Very quick.

rasch. Quick.

rauschend. Rustling, roaring.

recitative (recit.). A vocal style designed to imitate and emphasize the natural inflections of speech.

retenu. Held back.

revenir au Tempo. Return to the original tempo.

richtig. Correct (*richtige Lage,* correct pitch).

rigore di tempo. Strictness of tempo.

rigueur. Precision.

risoluto. Determined.

ritardando (rit., ritard.). Gradually slackening in speed.

ritenuto (riten.). Immediate reduction of speed.

rubato. A certain elasticity and flexibility of tempo, consisting of slight accelerandos and ritardandos according to the requirements of the musical expression.

ruhig. Quietly.

rullante. Rolling.

saltando (salt.). An indication to the string player to bounce the bow off the string by playing with short, quick bow-strokes.

sans timbre. Without snares.

scena vuota. Empty stage.

scherzando (scherz.). Playful.

schleppend. Dragging.

Schluss. Cadence, conclusion.

schmachtend. Languishing.

schnell. Fast.

schneller. Faster.

schon. Already.

scorrevole. Flowing, gliding.

sec, secco. Dry, simple.

seconda volta. The second time.

segue. (1) Continue to the next movement without pausing; (2) continue in the same manner.

sehr. Very.

semplicità. Simplicity.

sempre. Always, continually.

senza. Without.

sforzando, sforzato (sfz, sf). With sudden emphasis.

sfumato. Diminishing and fading away.

simile. In a similar manner.

Singstimme. Singing voice.

sino al. Up to the . . . (usually followed by a new tempo marking, or by a dotted line indicating a terminal point).

smorzando (smorz.). Dying away.

sofort. Immediately.

solo (s.). Executed by one performer.

sonator. Player (*uno sonator,* one player; *due sonatori,* two players).

sonné à la double 8va. Play the double octave.

sopra. Above; in piano music, used to indicate that one hand must pass above the other.

soprano (S.). The voice classification with the highest range.

sordino (sord.). Mute.

sostenendo, sostenuto. Sustained.

sotto voce. In an undertone, subdued, under the breath.

sourdine. Mute.

soutenu. Sustained.

spiccato. With a light bouncing motion of the bow.

spiritoso. In a spirited manner.

staccatissimo. Very staccato.

staccato (stacc.). Detached, separated, abruptly disconnected.

stentando, stentato (stent.). Delaying, retarding.

stesso movimento. The same basic pace.

stretto. In a non-fugal composition, indicates a concluding section at an increased speed.

stringendo (string.). Quickening.

subito (sub.). Suddenly, immediately.

sul. On the (as in *sul G,* on the G string).

suono. Sound, tone.

superius. In older music, the uppermost part.

sur. On.

suspendue. Suspended.

tacet. The instrument or vocal part so marked is silent.

tasto solo. In a continuo part, this indicates that only the string instrument plays; the chord-playing instrument is silent.

tempo primo (tempo I). At the original tempo.

tenor, tenore (T.). The highest male voice.

tenuto (ten.). Held, sustained.

tief. Deep, low.

tornando al tempo primo. Returning to the original tempo.

touch. Fingerboard (of a string instrument).

toujours. Always, continually.

tranquillo. Quietly, calmly.

tre corda (t.c.). Release the soft (or *una corda*) pedal of the piano.

tremolo (trem). On string instruments, a quick reiteration of the same tone, produced by a rapid up-and-down movement of the bow; also a rapid alternation between two different notes.

très. Very.

trill (tr.). The rapid alternation of a given note with the diatonic second above it. In a drum part it indicates rapid alternating strokes with two drumsticks.

triplum. In medieval polyphonic music, a voice part above the tenor.

troppo. Too much.

tutta la forza. Very emphatically.

tutti. Literally, "all"; usually means all the instruments in a given category as distinct from a solo part.

übergreifen. To overlap.

übertönend. Drowning out.

una corda (u.c.). With the "soft" pedal of the piano depressed.

und. And.

unison (unis.). The same notes or melody played by several instruments at the same pitch. Often used to emphasize that a phrase is not to be divided among several players.

verhallend. Fading away.

verklingen lassen. To let die away.

verlöschend. Extinguishing.

vierhändig. Four-hand piano music.

vif. Lively.

vivace. Quick, lively.

vivo. Lively.

voce. Voice (as in *colla voce,* a direction for the accompaniment to follow the solo part in tempo and expression).

voilà. There.

Vorhang auf. Curtain up.

Vorhang fällt, Vorhang zu. Curtain down.

voriges. Preceding.

Walzertempo. In the tempo of a waltz.

weg. Away, beyond.

weich. Mellow, smooth, soft.

weiter. Further, forward.

wie aus der Ferne. As if from afar.

wieder. Again.

wie oben. As above, as before.

wie zu Anfang dieser Szene. As at the beginning of this scene.

wüthend. Furiously.

zart. Tenderly, delicately.

Zeitmass. Tempo.

zögernd. Slower.

zu. The phrases *zu 2, zu 3* (etc.) indicate that the part is to be played in unison by 2, 3 (etc.) players.

zurückhaltend. Slackening in speed.

zurücktreten. To withdraw.

zweihändig. With two hands.

Index of Forms and Genres

A roman numeral following a title indicates a movement within the work named.